NCT's KOREAN VOCABULARY NOTE

Introductory remarks

NCT's KOREAN VOCABULARY NOTE consists of 450 basic Korean words and 200 basic sentences, helping beginners improve their Korean skills. It's a fun way to learn Korean with global K-pop idols NCT.

• The textbook consists of 5 chapter and 50 units in total.
• Vocabulary words are related to the themes of each unit and are based on a beginner level.

Global edition

NCT's KOREAN VOCABULARY NOTE

: 450 Korean Words and 200 Basic Expressions

1판 1쇄 인쇄 2025. 1. 8.
1판 1쇄 발행 2025. 1. 24.

지은이 KOYLABS(홈페이지 kokiri.co)

발행인 박강휘
편집 봉정하 디자인 정윤수 홍보 박은경 마케팅 이헌영, 이서연
필름캡쳐 & 이미지 보정 (주)브이에스에스
발행처 김영사
등록 1979년 5월 17일(제406-2003-036호)
주소 경기도 파주시 문발로 197(문발동) 우편번호 10881
전화 마케팅부 031)955-3100, 편집부 031)955-3200 | 팩스 031)955-3111

값은 뒤표지에 있습니다.
ISBN 979-11-94330-54-7 13710

홈페이지 www.gimmyoung.com　　　　블로그 blog.naver.com/gybook
인스타그램 instagram.com/gimmyoung　이메일 bestbook@gimmyoung.com

좋은 독자가 좋은 책을 만듭니다.
김영사는 독자 여러분의 의견에 항상 귀 기울이고 있습니다.

NCT와 배우는
기초 한국어

NCT's KOREAN VOCABULARY NOTE

Global Edition

Written by KOY LABS 감영사

Structure & Features

Unit Introduction

It introduces what the learners will study in each unit.

QR

Scan the QR code to access the KOKIRI app. Sign up after scanning the QR code to access relevant videos on the KOKIRI app.

New Words

Nine words related to the topic. After learning each word, practice in the blank space.

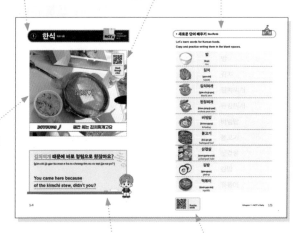

Episode Photo

Here are photos related to the topics found in NCT's original content videos.

Main Korean Expression

English translation, main Korean expression, and pronunciation.

QR

Practice word. If you scan the QR code, it will link you to the KOKIRI app.

Key Expressions

Learn four sentences
related to the
main topic. The
key expressions
in the sentences
(highlighted in green)
are explained below,
so study them once
more.

Exercise 2

After completing each unit, you will engage in activities
using the words and sentences you have learned.
Various activities such as writing, word puzzles, and
quizzes will be presented.

Exercise 1

Solve the exercises
while remembering
the new words
learned on the
previous page.

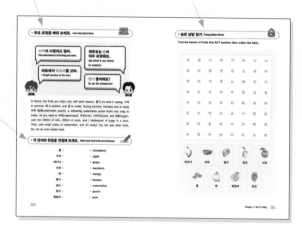

Exercise 3

Complete the task using
the NCT member character stickers.

Korean Culture

An aspect of Korean
culture is introduced.

Table of Contents

Vowels

The Korean language has 8 simple vowels and 13 complex vowels. The complex vowels are created by adding a stroke to simple vowel or combining simple vowels.

Simple Vowels	IPA	Romanization
ㅏ	[a]	a
ㅓ	[ə]	eo
ㅐ	[ɛ]	ae
ㅔ	[e]	e
ㅗ	[o]	o
ㅜ	[u]	u
ㅡ	[t]	eu
ㅣ	[i]	i

Combination of simple vowels and the /y/ sound.

Complex Vowels	IPA	Romanization
ㅑ	[ja]	ya
ㅕ	[jə]	yeo
ㅒ	[jɛ]	yae
ㅖ	[je]	ye
ㅛ	[jo]	yo
ㅠ	[ju]	yu

Combination of simple vowels and the /w/ sound.

Complex Vowels	IPA	Romanization
ㅘ	[wa]	wa
ㅝ	[wə]	wo
ㅙ	[wɛ]	wae
ㅞ	[we]	we
ㅚ	[we]	oe
ㅟ	[wi]	wi
ㅢ	[iy]	ui

* The vowels grouped in boxes have very similar pronunciations in practice.

Consonants

The Korean language has 19 consonants. Some are basic consonants, and others are their counterparts. They are created by adding a stroke to or repeating the basic consonant. The former is called "aspirated consonants" and the letter is called "tense consonant" or "double consonants."

These are consonants with basic sound.

Basic Consonants	IPA	Romanization
ㅂ	[p] / [b]	b
ㄷ	[t] / [d]	d
ㅅ	[s] / [ʃ]	s, sh
ㅈ	[ts] / [dz]	j
ㄱ	[k] / [g]	g
ㅁ	[m]	m
ㅇ	–	–

Stop the airflow briefly and release it with a burst, like a small explosion.

Aspirated Consonants	IPA	Romanization
ㅍ	[pʰ]	p
ㅌ	[tʰ]	t
–	–	–
ㅊ	[tsʰ]	ch
ㅋ	[kʰ]	k
ㄴ	[n]	n
ㅎ	[h]	h

Pronounce them intensely from the throat, without a burst of breath.

Tense Consonants	IPA	Romanization
ㅃ	[p]	pp
ㄸ	[t']	tt
ㅆ	[s'] / [ʃ']	ss, ssh
ㅉ	[ts']	jj
ㄲ	[k']	kk
ㄹ	[r] / [l]	r, l

Batchim

In writing, batchim can have various consonants, but there are only 7(ㄴ, ㄹ, ㅁ, ㅇ, ㅂ, ㄷ and ㄱ) pronunciations.

Batchim	IPA	Romanization
ㄴ	[n]	n
ㄹ	[l]	l
ㅁ	[m]	m
ㅇ	[ŋ]	ng

Batchim	Base Sound	IPA	Romanization
ㅂ, ㅍ	ㅂ	[p]	p
ㄷ, ㅌ, ㅅ, ㅆ, ㅈ, ㅊ	ㄷ	[t]	t
ㄱ, ㅋ, ㄲ	ㄱ	[k]	k

When ㅂ, ㄷ and ㄱ are batchim they are pronounced without a release of air, unlike the p, t and k sounds in the final position of English words such as "cup" "dot" and "book."

How to Make the Most of the App

Download the KOKIRI app by scanning the QR code,
and study with flashcards and videos featuring NCT members!

Step 1
Learn Vocabulary with NCT

Master essential Korean
vocabulary and example
sentences through fun videos
with NCT members.

Step 2
Word Card Game

Swipe through the cards
to memorize vocabulary.
You can also listen to
the Korean pronunciation.

Step 3
Review with Quizzes

Challenge yourself with
quizzes to memorize the words
you've learned. Any words
you miss will be saved to 'My
Bookmarks' for easy review!

Tap to save the word to
'My Bookmarks.'

CHAPTER 1

NCT's DAILY LIFE

① 한식 han-sik

DOYOUNG 해찬 씨는 김치찌개고요

김치찌개 때문에 바로 청팀으로 왔잖아요?

[gim-chi-jji-gae tta-mun-e ba-ro cheong-tim-eu-ro wat-jja-na-yo?]

**You came here because
of the kimchi stew, didn't you?**

Let's learn words for Korean foods. Trace and practice writing them in the blank spaces.

	밥 **[bap]** rice	밥
	김치 **[gim-chi]** kimchi	김치
	김치찌개 **[gim-chi-jji-gae]** kimchi stew	김치찌개
	된장찌개 **[doen-jang-jji-gae]** soybean paste stew	된장찌개
	비빔밥 **[bi-bim-ppap]** bibimbap	비빔밥
	불고기 **[bul-go-gi]** bulgogi	불고기
	삼겹살 **[sam-gyeop-ssal]** grilled pork belly	삼겹살
	김밥 **[gim-ppap]** gimbap	김밥
	떡볶이 **[tteok-ppo-kki]** tteokbokki	떡볶이

 Practice words

> ▸ **주요 표현을 배워 보세요.** Learn key expressions.

된장찌개를 만들었어요.
I made soybean paste stew.

떡볶이 좋아해.
I like tteokbokki.

삼겹살 같이 먹을까?
Shall we eat grilled pork belly together?

불고기 맛있어요.
Bulgogi is delicious.

Kimchi can be spicy food. You might not be able to eat kimchi at first because of its spiciness. In that case, try '백김치'(white kimchi). '백김치'(white kimchi) is not spicy enough for children to eat, so even first-time eaters can try it. Also, there are various kimchi-based dishes like 김치볶음밥(kimchi fried rice), 김치만두(kimchi dumpling) and 김치부침개(kimchi pancake), so you can enjoy variety flavors.

> ▸ **각 단어와 한글을 연결해 보세요.** Match each word to the correct Korean.

김밥 •	• tteokbokki
된장찌개 •	• gimbap
떡볶이 •	• grilled pork belly
불고기 •	• bulgogi
삼겹살 •	• kimchi stew
비빔밥 •	• kimchi
김치찌개 •	• bibimbap
김치 •	• rice
밥 •	• soybean paste stew

16

▸ **한식으로 급식표 만들기!** Creating a Korean School Meal Plan

Here's a monthly menu of favorite Korean dishes for NCT members.

일 SUN	월 MON	화 TUE	수 WED	목 THU	금 FRI	토 SAT
1주						
김치찌개						
2주						
3주						
4주						
5주						

Check through video

수박 맛 어때?

[su-bak mat eo-ttae?]

How is the watermelon?

Let's learn some words related to fruits. Trace the words and freely practice in the blank spaces.

	귤 [gyul] mandarin	귤
	딸기 [ttal-gi] strawberry	딸기
	배 [bae] pear	배
	사과 [sa-gwa] apple	사과
	복숭아 [bok-ssung-a] peach	복숭아
	수박 [su-bak] watermelon	수박
	망고 [mang-go] mango	망고
	포도 [po-do] grape	포도
	바나나 [ba-na-na] banana	바나나

Practice words

수박이 시원하고 달아.
This watermelon is refreshing and sweet.

제주도는 **귤**이 아주 유명해요.
Jeju Island is very famous for mandarin.

마트에서 **복숭아**를 샀어.
I bought peaches at the supermarket.

딸기 좋아해요?
Do you like strawberries?

In Korea, the fruits you enjoy vary with each season. 딸기 are best in spring, 수박 in summer, 배 in autumn, and 귤 in winter. During summer, Koreans love to enjoy 수박 화채(watermelon punch), a refreshing watermelon punch that's very easy to make. All you need is 수박(watermelon), 우유(milk), 사이다(soda), and 설탕(sugar). Just mix 500ml of milk, 200ml of soda, and 1 tablespoon of sugar in a bowl. Then add small cubes of watermelon and it's ready! You can add other fruits too, for an even tastier treat.

▸ **각 단어와 한글을 연결해 보세요.** Match each word to the correct Korean.

귤 ·   · strawberry

수박 ·   · apple

바나나 ·   · grape

사과 ·   · mandarin

배 ·   · mango

딸기 ·   · banana

포도 ·   · watermelon

망고 ·   · peach

복숭아 ·   · pear

▸ 숨은 낱말 찾기 Finding Hidden Words

Find the names of fruits that NCT members likes within the table.

과	일	나	라	가	바	나	나
귤	라	딸	면	방	고	재	마
마	바	기	먹	노	래	민	사
포	도	우	자	두	망	고	랑
체	리	유	파	인	애	플	해
도	수	박	소	금	사	빵	요
레	파	솔	라	시	과	태	배
미	감	복	숭	아	마	크	텐

바나나

수박

딸기

망고

사과

귤

배

복숭아

포도

NCT's
KOREAN
VOCABULARY
NOTE

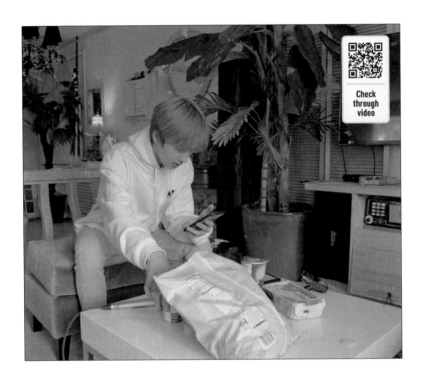

Check
through
video

올라가서 과자나 뜯어야지.

[ol-la-ga-seo gwa-ja-na ddeu-deo-ya-ji]

I'm going to go up
and open some snacks.

NCT
Korean
Vocabulary
note

▸ 새로운 단어 배우기 New Words

Let's learn some words related to snacks. Trace the words and freely practice in the blank spaces.

간식
[gan-sik]
snack

간식

과자
[gwa-ja]
biscuit

과자

커피
[keo-pi]
coffee

커피

케이크
[ke-i-keu]
cake

케이크

아이스크림
[a-i-seu-keu-lim]
ice cream

아이스크림

떡
[tteok]
rice cake

떡

빵
[ppang]
bread

빵

사탕
[sa-tang]
candy

사탕

초콜릿
[cho-kol-lit]
chocolate

초콜릿

Practice words

초콜릿 먹을래요?
Would you like some chocolate?

아침에 커피를 마셔.
I drink coffee in the morning.

이사 온 사람이 떡 줬어.
The new neighbor gave us rice cakes.

아이스크림 하나 줘.
Give me an ice cream.

Among Korean snacks, '떡' has been traditionally shared during happy or grateful occasions since ancient times. When someone moves into a new place, they give rice cakes to neighbors as a gesture of goodwill. The rice cake given at this time is usually '시루떡'(steamed rice cake) with red beans on top. It's believed that '팥'(red beans) ward off bad energy. People become closer by sharing rice cakes together.

▶ **각 단어와 한글을 연결해 보세요.** Match each word to the correct Korean.

아이스크림 •	• chocolate
떡 •	• coffee
빵 •	• candy
사탕 •	• ice cream
초콜릿 •	• snack
과자 •	• bread
케이크 •	• biscuit
커피 •	• rice cake
간식 •	• cake

▸ NCT 멤버들이 좋아하는 간식 To-eat List

Please write in Korean the snacks that NCT members want to eat.

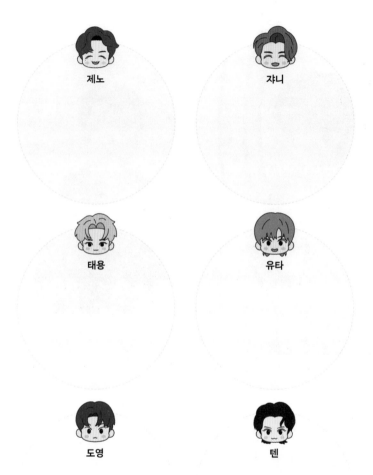

제노

쟈니

태용

유타

도영

텐

NCT's KOREAN VOCABULARY NOTE

XIAOJUN 너무 즐거워요

Check through video

NCT 다시 모인 거 너무 좋아해서 너무 **즐거워서**.

[en-si-ti da-si mo-in geo neo-mu jo-a-hae-seo neo-mu jeul-geo-wo-seo]

I've thoroughly enjoyed reuniting with NCT.

NCT Korean Vocabulary note

Let's learn some words related to feelings. Trace the words and frealy practice in the blank spaces.

	웃다 [ut-tta] laugh	웃다
	행복하다 [haeng-bok-ha-da] happy	행복하다
	슬프다 [seul-peu-da] sad	슬프다
	미안하다 [mi-an-ha-da] sorry	미안하다
	즐겁다 [jeul-geop-tta] pleasant	즐겁다
	편안하다 [pyeon-an-ha-da] comfortable	편안하다
	무섭다 [mu-seop-tta] scary	무섭다
	떨리다 [tteol-li-da] tremble	떨리다
	재미있다 [jae-mi-it-tta] funny	재미있다

Practice
words

If you want to express gratitude to someone, say '고마워요[gomawoyo]' or '고맙습니다[gomapseumnida]'. Similar expressions include '감사해요[gamsahaeyo]' or '감사합니다[gamsahamnida]'. Try using these greetings when you receive help from someone.

▸ **각 단어와 한글을 연결해 보세요.** Match each word to the correct Korean.

즐겁다 •	• happy
웃다 •	• funny
행복하다 •	• pleasant
편안하다 •	• sorry
재미있다 •	• tremble
슬프다 •	• scary
무섭다 •	• laugh
떨리다 •	• comfortable
미안하다 •	• sad

▸ 편지를 써 보세요. Try Writing a Letter.

Did you have a good day? Write a letter using words that express 'feelings' as shown below.

오늘 하루 잘 보내셨나요?

How was your day?

오늘 최고, 좋은 하루! 좋다

Today was the best, what a great day!

콘서트에서 여러분을 만나 행복해요. 행복하다

I'm happy to meet you all at the concert.

시즈니와 함께해서 정말 행복하고 좋아요.

I really like and am happy with NCTzens too.

Check through video

감기 걸리지 말고, 에어컨 세게 틀지 말고.

[gam-gi geol-li-ji-mal-go, e-eo-keon sse-ge teul-ji mal-go]

**Don't catch a cold,
don't leave the AC on too high.**

NCT Korean Vocabulary note

Let's learn some words related to the common cold. Trace the words and freely practice in the blank spaces.

	감기
	[gam-gi]
	cold

	기침
	[gi-chim]
	cough

	콧물
	[kon-mul]
	runny nose

	두통
	[du-tong]
	headache

	열
	[yeol]
	fever

	약
	[yak]
	medicine

	낫다
	[nat-tta]
	get better

	아프다
	[a-peu-da]
	ache

	조심하다
	[jo-sim-ha-da]
	be careful

 Practice words

▶ **주요 표현을 배워 보세요.** Learn key expressions.

감기 조심하세요.
Take care not to catch a cold.

머리가 아파요.
I have a headache.

약 먹고 좋아졌어.
I got better after taking medicine.

날씨가 추워서 콧물이 나요.
My nose is running because it's cold.

When it gets cold and people are likely to catch colds, people often say "감기 조심하세요[gamgi josimhaseyo]" as a greeting. This means "Take care of your health to avoid catching a cold." Similarly, people often say "건강 잘 챙기세요[geongang jal changgiseyo]"(Take care of your health).

▶ **각 단어와 한글을 연결해 보세요.** Match each word to the correct Korean.

약 •	• cold
열 •	• be careful
낫다 •	• cough
콧물 •	• ache
조심하다 •	• headache
감기 •	• fever
기침 •	• runny nose
아프다 •	• medicine
두통 •	• get better

▶ **댓글 쓰기!** **Writing Comments**

Read the post below and write a comment using the words you learned.

< 　　　　　　　**포스트**　　　　　　 ⤷ ⋮

👤 **NCT**　　　　　　　　　　　　　文A

어제 날씨가 추웠죠.
The weather was cold yesterday.
열이 나고 기침을 해요. 여러분, 감기 조심해요.
I have a fever and a cough. Everyone, be careful not to catch a cold.

1개의 추가 댓글

　　@ ＊＊
　　저도 감기에 걸려서 [　　　　　　]　　文A ⋮
　　그리고 [　　　　　　　]
　　[　　　　　　　　]
　　💬

댓글을 입력하세요.　　　　　　　↑

💬 10K+　　　　　　　　　　🔖

예문

머리가 아파요.　　　콧물이 나요.　　　약 먹고 쉬세요.
I have a headache.　My nose is running.　Take medicine and rest.

우리 강아지인 줄 알았어요.

[u-ri gang-a-ji-in jul a-ra-sseo-yo]

I thought you were talking about my dog.

Let's learn names of animals. Trace the words and freely practice in the blank spaces.

	강아지 [gang-a-ji] dog	강아지
	고양이 [go-yang-i] cat	고양이
	토끼 [to-kki] rabbit	토끼
	오리 [o-ri] duck	오리
	호랑이 [ho-rang-i] tiger	호랑이
	사자 [sa-ja] lion	사자
	코끼리 [ko-kki-ri] elephant	코끼리
	사슴 [sa-seum] deer	사슴
	돼지 [dwae-ji] pig	돼지

Practice words

> **나는 고양이를 키워.**
> I have a cat.

> **강아지와 산책했어요.**
> I took a walk with my dog.

> **나는 토끼처럼 귀여워.**
> I'm cute like a rabbit.

> **동물원에서 호랑이를 봤어요.**
> I saw a tiger at the zoo.

In Korea, there are alternative words for '강아지' and '고양이'. The sound a dog makes is '멍멍[meongmeong]', and a cat's sound is '야옹[yaong]'. So using these sounds, people sometimes call dogs '멍멍이[meongmeongi]' and cats '야옹이[yaongi]' instead.

▸ **각 단어와 한글을 연결해 보세요.** Match each word to the correct Korean.

고양이 •   • tiger

사슴 •   • duck

강아지 •   • pig

돼지 •   • lion

토끼 •   • dog

호랑이 •   • elephant

오리 •   • rabbit

사자 •   • cat

코끼리 •   • deer

▸ 동물! 초성 퀴즈 Animal Initial Sound Quiz

Match the initials to find the name of the animal that resembles each member.

도영 ㅌ ㄲ

재현 ㄱ ㅇ ㅇ

정우 ㄱ ㅇ ㅈ

마크 ㅊ ㅌ

양양 ㅇ

해찬 ㄱ

보기

토끼	고양이	강아지	치타	양	곰
rabbit	cat	dog	cheetah	sheep	bear

Check through video

귀도 따뜻하고 목도 따뜻하고.

[gwi-do tta-tteu-ta-go mok-do tta-tteu-ta-go]

Ears are warm

and the neck is warm.

NCT Korean Vocabulary note

▶ 새로운 단어 배우기 New Words

Let's learn expressions about weather. Trace the words and freely practice in the blank spaces.

	따뜻하다 [tta-tteu-ta-da] warm	따뜻하다
	흐리다 [heu-ri-da] cloudy	흐리다
	나쁘다 [na-ppeu-da] bad	나쁘다
	맑다 [mak-tta] clear	맑다
	좋다 [jo-ta] fine / good	좋다
	쌀쌀하다 [ssal-ssal-ha-da] chilly	쌀쌀하다
	춥다 [chup-tta] cold	춥다
	덥다 [deop-tta] hot	덥다
	습하다 [seu-pa-da] humid	습하다

Practice words

날씨가 좋아.
The weather is good.

너무 더워서 아이스크림 샀어.
I bought ice cream because it was too hot.

날씨가 추워서 옷 입었어.
I dressed warmly because it's cold outside.

비가 와서 습해.
It's humid because it's raining.

In Korea, there's a term '여우비'(sun shower) among weather expressions. It combines the words '여우'(fox) and '비'. '여우'(fox) are known for their quick movements, appearing and disappearing in the blink of an eye. Therefore, a brief shower that occurs on a sunny day is called '여우비'(sun shower), as it appears and disappears quickly like a fox.

▸ **각 단어와 한글을 연결해 보세요.** Match each word to the correct Korean.

흐리다 •	• chilly
습하다 •	• hot
따뜻하다 •	• cloudy
쌀쌀하다 •	• warm
맑다 •	• cold
춥다 •	• humid
덥다 •	• clear
좋다 •	• fine / good
나쁘다 •	• bad

‣ 날씨가 어때요? NCT 멤버들에게 이야기해 주세요.

How's the weather? Tell NCT members about it.

좋다
fine, good

나쁘다
bad

맑다
clear

흐리다
cloudy

따뜻하다
warm

덥다
hot

쌀쌀하다
chilly

춥다
cool

오늘 날씨가 　　　　　　　.

날씨가 　　　　　　　.

하늘이 　　　　　　　.

해가 비쳐서 　　　　　　　.

날씨가 　　　　　　　.

바람이 불어 　　　　　　　.

눈도 오고 너무 　　　　　　　.

오늘 진짜 다 부수고 가.

[o-neul jin-jja da bu-su-go ga]

Today just break everything.

Let's learn expressions about time. Trace the words and freely practice in the blank spaces.

M T W T F 1 2 3 4 5	**어제** [eo-je] yesterday	어제
M T W T F 1 2 3 4 5	**오늘** [o-neul] today	오늘
M T W T F 1 2 3 4 5	**내일** [nae-il] tomorrow	내일
(calendar)	**지난주** [ji-nan-ju] last week	지난주
(calendar)	**이번 주** [i-beon ju] this week	이번 주
(calendar)	**다음 주** [da-eum ju] next week	다음 주
2024 작년 2026 2025	**작년** [jang-nyeon] last year	작년
2024 2026 2025 올해	**올해** [ol-hae] this year	올해
2026 2024 내년 2025	**내년** [nae-nyeon] next year	내년

Practice words

어제 책을 샀어요.
I bought a book yesterday.

오늘 시간 있어?
Do you have time today?

내일 영화 볼 거야.
I'm going to watch a movie tomorrow.

다음 주에 여행 가요.
I'm going on a trip next week.

There are special words for counting days in Korean. One day is '하루'(one day), two days is '이틀'(two days), three days is '사흘'(three days), and four days is '나흘'(four days). So when asking someone about their day, you might say "오늘 하루 어땠어요?"(How was your day?).

▶ **각 단어와 한글을 연결해 보세요.** Match each word to the correct Korean.

어제 •   • tomorrow

올해 •   • next week

작년 •   • today

내일 •   • this year

이번 주 •   • yesterday

오늘 •   • next year

지난주 •   • this week

내년 •   • last year

다음 주 •   • last week

‣ NCTzen의 하고 싶은 일 To-do List!

Using the examples and expressions learned earlier, make a list of the things you want to do.

sample 어제

- [ ] 운동 Exercise
- [ ] 친구 만나기 Meeting Friends
- [ ] 노래 부르기 Singing
- [ ] 잠자기 Sleeping
- [ ] 독서 Reading
- [ ] 휴식 Rest

오늘

- [ ]
- [ ]
- [ ]
- [ ]
- [ ]
- [ ]

내일

- [ ]
- [ ]
- [ ]
- [ ]
- [ ]
- [ ]

지난주

- [ ]
- [ ]
- [ ]
- [ ]
- [ ]
- [ ]

이번 주

- [ ]
- [ ]
- [ ]
- [ ]
- [ ]
- [ ]

다음 주

- [ ]
- [ ]
- [ ]
- [ ]
- [ ]
- [ ]

작년

- [ ]
- [ ]
- [ ]
- [ ]
- [ ]
- [ ]

올해

- [ ]
- [ ]
- [ ]
- [ ]
- [ ]
- [ ]

내년

- [ ]
- [ ]
- [ ]
- [ ]
- [ ]
- [ ]

Check through video

나 **아침**에 커피랑 같이 먹어.

[na a-chim-e keo-pi-rang ga-chi meo-geo]

NCT Korean Vocabulary note

I eat it with coffee in the morning.

Let's learn expressions about time. Trace the words and freely practice in the blank spaces.

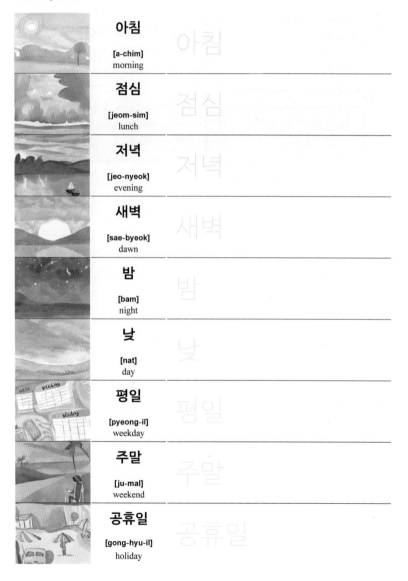

	아침
	[a-chim] morning

	점심
	[jeom-sim] lunch

	저녁
	[jeo-nyeok] evening

	새벽
	[sae-byeok] dawn

	밤
	[bam] night

	낮
	[nat] day

	평일
	[pyeong-il] weekday

	주말
	[ju-mal] weekend

	공휴일
	[gong-hyu-il] holiday

Practice words

아침에 일어나서
운동해요.
I exercise after waking up
in the morning.

오후에 약속이 있어.
I have an appointment in the afternoon.

저녁에 홍대에서 만날까?
Shall we meet at Hongdae
in the evening?

주말에 뭐 해요?
What are you doing
this weekend?

In Korea, while "안녕하세요[annyeonghaseyo]"(Hello) is commonly used as a greeting, "밥 먹었어요[bap meogeosseoyo]?"(Did you eat?) is commonly used to ask if you have eaten rice. This can be used regardless of time. You can replace 'rice' with '아침', '점심', or '저녁'. Here, these words refer to '식사'(meals) rather than times of day. "저녁 먹었어요[jeonyeok meogeosseoyo]?" means "Did you have dinner?"

▶ **각 단어와 한글을 연결해 보세요.** Match each word to the correct Korean.

점심 •   • evening

새벽 •   • weekend

아침 •   • holiday

주말 •   • dawn

공휴일 •   • night

저녁 •   • morning

밤 •   • lunch

낮 •   • weekday

평일 •   • day

Find the words below hidden in the puzzle.

보기

아침	저녁	새벽	밤
점심	주말	공휴일	평일

가	나	다	라	마	바	사	월	요	일
엔	시	티	콘	서	트	아	침	창	가
수	산	들	바	람	저	녁	약	그	림
요	금	밤	양	갱	보	이	속	편	가
일	나	는	새	벽	비	주	시	지	족
고	눈	부	신	하	늘	말	간	구	름
구	평	사	원	무	지	개	점	심	밥
마	일	봄	소	풍	공	휴	일	식	사
화	요	일	모	래	시	계	가	을	날
앨	범	누	리	집	한	국	어	공	부

NCT's KOREAN VOCABULARY NOTE

JISUNG   나 연습 못했어 진짜

많이 먹었다.

[ma-ni meo-geot-tta]

We ate a lot now.

50

Let's learn some words related to activities. Trace the words and freely practice in the blank spaces.

	보다 [bo-da] see	보다
	듣다 [deut-tta] hear / listen	듣다
	말하다 [mal-ha-da] say / tell	말하다
	먹다 [meok-tta] eat	먹다
	가다 [ga-da] go	가다
	오다 [o-da] come	오다
	걷다 [geot-tta] walk	걷다
	자다 [ja-da] sleep	자다
	읽다 [ik-tta] read	읽다

Practice words

노래 듣고 있어요.
I'm listening to music.

커피 마시고 책 읽었어.
I drank coffee and read a book.

집에 가는 중이에요.
I'm on my way home.

아까 과자 먹었어.
I ate snacks earlier.

When reading a book, newspaper or magazine we say "책을/신문을/잡지를 읽어 요"(I read a book/newspaper/magazine). However, Koreans often use '봐요' in place of '읽어요'. So we say "책을/신문을/잡지를 봐요"(I read a book/newspaper/ magazine).

▸ **각 단어와 한글을 연결해 보세요.** Match each word to the correct Korean.

듣다 •   • go

말하다 •   • listen / hear

가다 •   • come

보다 •   • sleep

읽다 •   • walk

먹다 •   • see

자다 •   • say / tell

걷다 •   • read

오다 •   • eat

‣ NCT의 하루 스케줄 NCT's Daily Schedule

Using the example below, create a daily schedule for NCT members.

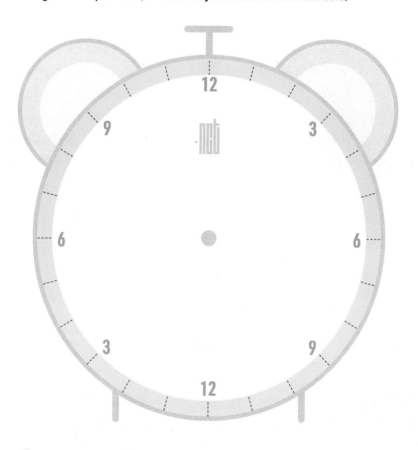

일어나기 getting up   음악 듣기 listening to music   운동하기 exercise

산책 walk   유튜브 보기 watching YouTube   잠자기 sleeping

카페 가기 going to a cafe   책 읽기 reading books   밥 먹기 eating

CHAPTER 2

NCT's LIFESTYLE

Check through video

근데 지성이는 뭐, 카페도 하고 공부도 하는 거야?

[geun-de Ji-seong-i-neun mwo, ka-pe-do ha-go gong-bu-do ha-neun geo-ya?]

Are you working at this cafe and studying too, JISUNG?

♡ NCT Korean Vocabulary note

Let's learn words related to places. Trace the words and freely practice in the blank spaces.

이미지	단어	발음 / 뜻	연습
	공원	[gong-won] park	공원
	영화관	[yeong-hwa-gwan] cinema	영화관
	놀이동산	[no-li-dong-san] amusement park	놀이동산
	매표소	[mae-pyo-so] ticket office	매표소
	미용실	[mi-yong-sil] hair salon	미용실
	노래방	[no-rae-bang] singing room	노래방
	식당	[sik-ttang] restaurant	식당
	카페	[ka-pe] cafe	카페
	고향	[go-hyang] hometown	고향

Practice words

놀이공원에 놀러 갔어요.
I went to the amusement park.

내가 좋아하는 카페야.
This is my favorite cafe.

공원에서 산책할까요?
Shall we take a walk in the park?

노래방 같이 가자.
Let's go to the singing room.

When you want to order food at a restaurant, say "여기요"(Excuse me) or "저기요"(Excuse me). These are words to call staff. "여기"(here) refers to a place close to the speaker, while "저기"(there) refers to a place far from the speaker.

▸ **각 단어와 한글을 연결해 보세요.** Match each word to the correct Korean.

노래방 •   • ticket office

공원 •   • hair salon

놀이공원 •   • cinema

식당 •   • cafe

미용실 •   • restaurant

고향 •   • amusement park

영화관 •   • park

매표소 •   • singing room

카페 •   • hometown

코인 노래방

coin singing room

Coin singing rooms, or "coin noraebang" in Korean, are popular entertainment spots in South Korea where individuals or groups can enjoy singing in a private setting. These venues are named for their unique payment system, where instead of paying for a fixed amount of time, users insert coins to activate the machine for a set number of songs or minutes. This makes it a more affordable and flexible option for those who just want to sing a few songs without committing to an hour or more.

Coin singing rooms are typically equipped with a sound system, microphone, remote control for song selection, and a screen displaying the lyrics. The song libraries are extensive, including both Korean and international hits. They are often found in busy areas with lots of foot traffic like shopping districts and near universities, making them an easy and accessible option for spontaneous entertainment.

와 진짜 뭔가 맛있어 보인다

돼지고기 32인분이요.

[dwae-ji-go-gi 32-in-bun-i-yo]

NCT Korean Vocabulary note

Thirty-two servings of pork is here.

Let's learn cooking ingredients. Trace the words and freely practice in the blank spaces.

	소고기 [so-go-gi] beef	소고기
	돼지고기 [dwae-ji-go-gi] pork	돼지고기
	계란 [gye-ran] eggs	계란
	두부 [du-bu] tofu	두부
	소금 [so-geum] salt	소금
	된장 [doen-jang] soybean paste	된장
	고추장 [go-chu-jang] hot pepper paste	고추장
	설탕 [seol-tang] sugar	설탕
	간장 [gan-jang] soy sauce	간장

Practice words

계란 있어?
Do you have eggs?

김치찌개에 돼지고기 넣자.
Let's put pork in the kimchi stew.

냉장고에 고추장 없어요.
There's no hot pepper paste in the refrigerator.

소금 더 넣을까요?
Should I add more salt?

When talking about Korean food, we say '한식[hansik]'(Korean food). A representative '한식' dish is '비빔밥'(bibimbap). '비빔'(mixing) comes from '비비다'(mix) meaning to mix various ingredients together. So '비빔밥' is eaten by '나물'(seasoned vegetables) with '계란', '고추장', and '참기름'.

▶ **각 단어와 한글을 연결해 보세요.** Match each word to the correct Korean.

소고기 •　　　　　　　 • sugar

계란 •　　　　　　　 • soy sauce

돼지고기 •　　　　　　　 • beef

두부 •　　　　　　　 • soybean paste

된장 •　　　　　　　 • pork

고추장 •　　　　　　　 • eggs

간장 •　　　　　　　 • salt

설탕 •　　　　　　　 • tofu

소금 •　　　　　　　 • hot pepper paste

김밥 만들기

Making Gimbap

① **김을 펼쳐 주세요.**
Spread out the seaweed.

② **밥에 소금과 참기름을 넣고 섞어 주세요.**
그리고 그 밥을 김 위에 펴 주세요.
Add salt and sesame oil to the rice and mix well.
Then spread the rice on top of the seaweed.

③ **당근, 햄, 단무지 등 재료를 밥 위에 올려 주세요.**
Place ingredients such as carrots, ham, and pickled radish on top of the rice.

④ **재료가 나오지 않게 김을 돌돌 잘 말아 주세요.**
Roll the seaweed tightly so that the ingredients do not come out.

⑤ **먹기 좋은 크기로 썰어 맛있게 먹어요.**
Cut it into bite-sized pieces and enjoy your meal.

Check through video

이것만 굽고.

[i-geon-man gup-kko]

I'll just grill this.

Let's learn some cooking verbs. Trace the words and freely practice in the blank spaces.

	자르다 [ja-reu-da] to chop	자르다
	썰다 [sseol-da] to slice	썰다
	깎다 [kkak-tta] to peel	깎다
	끓이다 [kkeu-li-da] to boil	끓이다
	찌다 [jji-da] to steam	찌다
	튀기다 [twi-gi-da] to fry	튀기다
	굽다 [gup-tta] to grill	굽다
	볶다 [bok-tta] stir-fried	볶다
	넣다 [neo-ta] to add	넣다

Practice words

당근을 자르세요.
Cut the carrots.

먼저 물을 끓이세요.
First boil the water.

감자 볶았어요?
Have you stir-fried the potatoes?

오이를 얇게 썰어 주세요.
Please slice the cucumber thinly.

'끓이다' is used when heating food while cooking. However, it can also refer to completed dishes. Like "라면을 끓였다[ramyeon-eul kkulyeotta]"(I cooked ramyeon) doesn't mean the ramyeon is still boiling, but rather means "라면을 완성했다 [ramyeon-eul wanseonghaetta]"(The ramyeon is ready).

▸ **각 단어와 한글을 연결해 보세요.** Match each word to the correct Korean.

자르다 ·   · to add

찌다 ·   · to slice

넣다 ·   · to boil

굽다 ·   · stir-fried

볶다 ·   · to peel

썰다 ·   · to chop

끓이다 ·   · to steam

깎다 ·   · to grill

튀기다 ·   · to fry

▸ 재민과 함께하는 요리교실 Cooking Class!

Let's make delicious soy sauce egg rice with JAEMIN.

간장 계란밥

ganjang gyeranbap

재료

따뜻한 밥 1공기, 계란 1개, 간장 1스푼(T), 참기름 1스푼(T)
1 bowl of warm rice, 1 egg, 1 tablespoon(T) of soy sauce, 1 tablespoon(T) of sesame oil

① **따뜻한 밥 1공기를 준비해 주세요.**
Prepare 1 bowl of warm rice.

② **계란 1개를 프라이해 주세요.**
Fry 1 egg.
계란을 좋아한다면 2~3개를 준비해 주세요.
If you like eggs, prepare 2-3 eggs.
계란을 만진 전후로는 손을 꼭 씻어 주세요.
Be sure to wash your hands before and after handling eggs.

③ **밥 위에 계란 프라이를 올리고 간장 1스푼(T)과**
참기름 1스푼(T)을 넣은 후 비벼 주세요.
Place the fried egg on top of the rice, add 1 tablespoon(T) of soy sauce and
1 tablespoon(T) of sesame oil, and mix well.

④ **여기에 사랑 1스푼 정성 1스푼을 첨가해 주면 더욱 맛있어요.**
Adding 1 tablespoon of love and 1 tablespoon of sincerity will make it even more
delicious.

아기 기상청 **재민**

이렇게 시즈니들의 열기로 <u>봄</u>이
빠르게 오고 있다고 하는데요.

[i-reo-ke si-jeu-ni-deu-rui yeol-gi-ro bo-mi
ppa-reu-ge o-go it-tta-go ha-neun-de-yo]

Spring has been approaching fast
with the enthusiasm of NCTzen.

NCT
Korean
Vocabulary
note

Let's learn words related to nature. Trace the words and freely practice in the blank spaces.

	봄 [bom] spring	
	구름 [gu-reum] cloud	
	꽃 [kkot] flower	
	나무 [na-mu] tree	
	바다 [ba-da] sea	
	바람 [ba-ram] wind	
	눈 [nun] snow	
	비 [bi] rain	
	하늘 [ha-neul] sky	

Practice words

바람이 불어요.
The wind is blowing.

크리스마스에 눈이 와요.
It snows on Christmas.

하늘이 너무 예뻐.
The sky is so beautiful.

봄이 와서 따뜻해.
Spring has come and it's warm.

When describing '눈' or '비' falling, use '오다'(come). Say '눈이 와(요)(Snow comes), 비가 와(요)(Rain comes)'. '내리다'(fall) is also commonly used, so you can say '눈이 내려(요)(Snow falls), 비가 내려(요)(Rain falls)'.

▸ **각 단어와 한글을 연결해 보세요.** Match each word to the correct Korean.

꽃 •   • spring

바람 •   • cloud

바다 •   • sky

나무 •   • sea

눈 •   • flower

비 •   • wind

하늘 •   • rain

구름 •   • tree

봄 •   • snow

Below is a text that describes the four seasons in Korea. Use the words provided to describe the seasons in your country.

한국의 사계절은 최고예요.

봄에는 꽃이 피고 하늘이 예뻐요.

여름에는 덥지만 바다에서 수영할 수 있어 좋아요.

가을은 단풍을 보고 겨울에는 눈을 봐요.

시즈니와 함께 사계절을 보고 싶어요.

| 사계절 four seasons | 여름 summer | 가을 autumn |
| 단풍 maple | 겨울 winter | |

혼란스런 세계관
막 스파이더맨이야

좀비들이 막 빌딩을 진짜 올라와.

[jom-bi-deu-li mak bil-ding-eul jin-jja ol-la-wa]

The zombies are crawling
up the building for real.

NCT
Korean
Vocabulary
note

▶ 새로운 단어 배우기 New Words

Let's learn some words related to the city. Trace the words and freely practice in the blank spaces.

빌딩
[bil-ding]
building

빌딩

도로/길
[do-ro/gil]
road/street

도로/길

신호등
[sin-ho-deung]
traffic light

신호등

정류장
[jeong-nyu-jang]
bus stop

정류장

편의점
[pyeo-nui-jeom]
convenience store

편의점

지하철역
[ji-ha-cheol-ryeok]
subway station

지하철역

횡단보도
[hoeng-dan-bo-do]
crosswalk

횡단보도

아파트
[a-pa-teu]
apartment

아파트

다리
[da-ri]
bridge

다리

Practice
words

지하철에 사람이 많아요.
There are many people on the subway.

아파트에 살고 있어요.
I live in an apartment.

지금 정류장 앞이야.
I'm in front of the bus stop now.

편의점 갈래?
Shall we go to the convenience store?

At Korean '버스 정류장[beoseu jeongnyujang]'(bus stops), you can check bus arrival times and available seats. This makes it convenient to know bus information in advance. There are also heated seats and heated shelters at stops to avoid the cold. Some bus stops in Gangnam even have phone charging stations, so try visiting them.

▸ **각 단어와 한글을 연결해 보세요.** Match each word to the correct Korean.

지하철역 •   • apartment

도로 / 길 •   • crosswalk

아파트 •   • subway station

횡단보도 •   • road

정류장 •   • traffic light

다리 •   • building

신호등 •   • bus stop

빌딩 •   • bridge

편의점 •   • convenience store

▶ 숨은 낱말 찾기 Finding Hidden Words

Find the words below hidden in the puzzle.

보기

빌딩	횡단보도	정류장	편의점
도로	아파트	다리	신호등

한	강	에	서	유	람	선	을	타	요
엔	시	티	아	파	트	편	의	점	한
오	렌	지	색	물	감	지	는	울	강
렌	지	빌	딩	통	각	순	간	시	다
지	유	니	버	스	정	류	장	티	리
서	야	구	장	사	이	로	골	인	오
울	도	회	사	람	바	람	에	신	렌
그	로	이	도	시	가	준	답	호	지
림	불	이	나	횡	단	보	도	등	색
너	와	같	이	석	양	속	에	서	밤

기차에서 찍은 건가요?

[gi-cha-e-seo jji-geun geon-ga-yo?]

Did you take this on the train?

Let's learn words for transportation. Trace the words and freely practice in the blank spaces.

배
[bae]
boat
배

기차
[gi-cha]
train
기차

버스
[beo-seu]
bus
버스

비행기
[bi-haeng-gi]
airplane
비행기

택시
[taek-si]
taxi
택시

공항
[gong-hang]
airport
공항

자전거
[ja-jeon-geo]
bicycle
자전거

자동차
[ja-dong-cha]
car
자동차

터미널
[teo-mi-neol]
terminal
터미널

Practice
words

공항 가는 길이에요.
I'm on my way to the airport.

우리 택시 탈까요?
Shall we take a taxi?

공원에서 자전거 타자.
Let's ride bikes in the park.

버스 정류장 앞에서 기다려.
Wait in front of the bus stop.

When using buses, subways, taxis, etc. in Korea, it's convenient to have a '교통 카드'(transportation card). There's a rechargeable transportation card commonly called '티머니'(T-money). If you buy and charge this card, you can travel around Korea very conveniently. There's a transfer system for buses and subways which makes transportation costs cheaper, and the cards come in various designs so you can choose one you like.

▸ **각 단어와 한글을 연결해 보세요.** Match each word to the correct Korean.

기차 •	• terminal
배 •	• airport
비행기 •	• car
버스 •	• train
택시 •	• boat
공항 •	• bicycle
자전거 •	• bus
자동차 •	• airplane
터미널 •	• taxi

▸ 나는 무엇일까요? Guess what?

Read the instructions below and guess what transportation the NCT members used. Choose from the pictures below.

보기

| 배 | 기차 | 버스 | 택시 | 자전거 |

1단계 나는 무엇일까요?
What I am?

2단계 혼자 타기도 하고 친구와 타기도 해요.
You can ride it alone or with a friend.

3단계 바퀴가 있어요.
It has wheels.

4단계 보통은 바퀴가 2개예요.
It usually has two wheels.

정답: _____

《(아이디)카드 나왔어~

카드 **나왔어!**

[ka-deu na-wa-sseo]

Got a card!

80

Let's learn some words related to shopping. Trace the words and freely practice in the blank spaces.

마트
[ma-teu]
mart

마트

현금
[hyeon-geum]
cash

현금

시장
[si-jang]
market

시장

계산하다
[gye-san-ha-da]
calculate

계산하다

할인
[ha-lin]
discount

할인

봉투
[bong-tu]
bag

봉투

쇼핑카트
[syo-ping-ka-teu]
shopping cart

쇼핑카트

카드
[ka-deu]
card

카드

영수증
[yeong-su-jeung]
receipt

영수증

Practice words

계산해 주세요.
Check, please.

영수증 주세요.
Please give me the receipt.

카드 챙겼어?
Did you bring your card?

봉투에 넣어 주세요.
Put it in the bag, please.

At the '마트', if you're curious about an item's price, ask "얼마예요[eolmayeyo]?" (How much is it?). If you don't have '현금', you can ask if '카드' payment is possible by saying "카드 결제돼요?"(Can you take a credit card?). If you think something is expensive at the market, you can say "깎아 주세요"(Please give me a discount). They might lower the price, but remember this varies by store.

▸ **각 단어와 한글을 연결해 보세요.** Match each word to the correct Korean.

마트 •   • receipt

현금 •   • card

시장 •   • shopping cart

계산하다 •   • bag

할인 •   • mart

봉투 •   • cash

쇼핑카트 •   • market

카드 •   • calculate

영수증 •   • discount

광장시장

Gwangjangsijang(Gwangjang Market)

서울연구네이터서비스 https://data.si.re.kr

Gwangjang Market: A Vibrant Traditional Marketplace in Seoul

Gwangjang Market is one of the most representative traditional markets in Seoul, offering foreign tourists a unique opportunity to experience Korean culture and traditions. At this lively market, visitors can explore a diverse array of traditional Korean foods and products, immersing themselves in the bustling atmosphere.

History and Transformation of Gwangjang Market

Gwangjang Market was established in 1905, making it over 100 years old, and is one of the oldest traditional markets in Seoul.

In recent years, Gwangjang Market has undergone modernization and tourism development efforts, transforming it into a new and vibrant destination.

Gwangjang Market location:

Jongno 5-ga Station Exit 8 on Seoul Subway Line 1, Euljiro 4-ga Station Exit 4 on Subway Lines 2 and 5

Check through video

좋은 데 예약했거든요.

[jo-eun de ye-ya-kaet-geo-deun-yo]

I reserved a nice restaurant.

NCT Korean Vocabulary note

Let's learn some words related to accommodation. Trace the words and freely practice in the blank spaces.

예약하다
[ye-ya-ka-da]
make a reservation

예약하다

맡기다
[mat-kki-da]
leave

맡기다

조식
[jo-sik]
breakfast

조식

묵다
[muk-tta]
stay

묵다

빈방
[bin-bang]
vacancy

빈방

짐
[jim]
luggage

짐

싸다
[ssa-da]
pack

싸다

풀다
[pul-da]
unpack

풀다

취소하다
[chwi-so-ha-da]
cancel

취소하다

Practice words

빈방 있어요?
Do you have any vacancy?

어제 숙소 예약했어요.
I made a hotel reservation yesterday.

조식 먹으러 가자.
Let's eat breakfast.

먼저 짐 맡길까?
Should we leave our luggage first?

If it's your first time traveling to Korea, there's a '숙소' I'd like to recommend. It's a '한옥 스테이'(Hanok Stay) where you can experience staying in a traditional Korean house called a '한옥'(Hanok). '한옥' is a traditional Korean house, and staying there allows you to experience Korean traditional culture and appreciate Korean beauty. You can experience Korean ondol(floor heating) culture, traditional tea ceremonies, and get closer to Korean culture.

▸ **각 단어와 한글을 연결해 보세요.** Match each word to the correct Korean.

취소하다 •	• breakfast
풀다 •	• stay
싸다 •	• cancel
예약하다 •	• pack
묵다 •	• unpack
조식 •	• make a reservation
맡기다 •	• luggage
빈방 •	• leave
짐 •	• vacancy

Please answer the questions below.

1. **NCT 127 정규 6집에 수록된 곡이 아닌 것은?**
   Which song was not included in NCT 127's 6th full Album?

   ① 삐그덕 (Walk)

   ② 오렌지색 물감 (Orange Seoul)

   ③ 영화처럼 (Can't Help Myself)

   ④ 우산 (Love Song)

   ⑤ Pricey

   이름 Name:

   점수 Score:

2. **NCT 127의 정규 5집 Fact Check(불가사의; 不可思議) 뮤직비디오의 촬영지는 어디 인가요?** Where was the music video for NCT 127's 5th full Album 'Fact Check' filmed?

   ① 덕수궁 Deoksugung Palace

   ② 경복궁 Gyeongbokgung Palace

   ③ 창경궁 Changgyeonggung Palace

   ④ 서울숲 Seoul Forest

   ⑤ 창덕궁 Changdeokgung Palace

3. **다음 중 NCT 유닛이 아닌 것은?**
   Which of the following is not a NCT unit?

   ① NCT DREAM

   ② NCT 도재정

   ③ NCT 127

   ④ WayV

   ⑤ 불가사의 Bulgasaeui

4. **다음 중 NCT DREAM 정규 앨범이 아닌 것은?**
   Which of the following is not a NCT DREAM's full album?

   ① ISTJ

   ② Glitch Mode

   ③ 맛 (Hot Sauce)

   ④ DREAMSCAPE

   ⑤ DREAM( )SCAPE

5. **WayV의 멤버는 몇 명인가요?** _____

   How many members are in WayV?

게임이 끝났어요.

[ge-i-mi kkeun-na-sseo-yo]

The game is over.

▶ 새로운 단어 배우기 New Words

Let's learn some words related to hobbies. Trace the words and freely practice in the blank spaces.

	영화 감상 **[yeong-hwa gam-sang]** watching movies	영화 감상
	독서 **[dok-sseo]** reading	독서
	운동 **[un-dong]** exercise	운동
	음악 **[eu-mak]** music	음악
	사진 **[sa-jin]** photography	사진
	그림 **[geu-rim]** drawing	그림
	게임 **[ge-im]** game	게임
	등산 **[deung-san]** hiking	등산
	취미 **[chwi-mi]** hobby	취미

 Practice words

취미가 뭐예요?
What's your hobby?

게임을 좋아해서 자주 해요.
I like games so I do it often.

주말마다
등산하러 가.
I go hiking every weekend.

사진 찍는 것을 좋아해.
I like taking pictures.

When you're curious about someone's hobby, ask "취미가 뭐예요?". A similar formal expression is "취미가 어떻게 되세요?" If you're curious about what someone likes, you can also ask 'N 좋아해요?'(Do you like N?). You can replace N with words like '게임, 사진, 등산' etc.

▸ **각 단어와 한글을 연결해 보세요.** Match each word to the correct Korean.

취미 •	• music
등산 •	• reading
게임 •	• photography
영화 감상 •	• hobby
독서 •	• watching movies
운동 •	• drawing
사진 •	• game
음악 •	• hiking
그림 •	• exercise

What are NCT members' hobbies? Write them in the space below.

Nct Hobby Report

NAME	
재민	
HOBBY	
사진	

NAME	
쿤	
HOBBY	

NAME	
해찬	
HOBBY	

NAME	
태용	
HOBBY	

NAME	
윈윈	
HOBBY	

NAME	
텐	
HOBBY	

NAME	
도영	
HOBBY	

NAME	
유타	
HOBBY	

NAME	
재현	
HOBBY	

NAME	
쟈니	
HOBBY	

Check through video

수영하자!

[su-yeong-ha-ja]

Let's swim!

Let's learn about different sports. Trace the words and freely practice in the blank spaces.

	축구	축구
	[chuk-kku] soccer	
	농구	농구
	[nong-gu] basketball	
	야구	야구
	[ya-gu] baseball	
	스키	스키
	[seu-ki] skiing	
	배드민턴	배드민턴
	[bae-deu-min-teon] badminton	
	테니스	테니스
	[te-ni-seu] tennis	
	수영	수영
	[su-yeong] swimming	
	태권도	태권도
	[tae-gwon-do] taekwondo	
	볼링	볼링
	[bol-ling] bowling	

Practice words

집에서 축구 경기를 봐요.
I watch soccer games at home.

야구 보러 갈래요?
Would you like to go watch baseball?

같이 테니스 치자.
Let's play tennis together.

친구들과 스키 타러 가.
I go skiing with my friends.

Korea has a unique '야구' cheering culture. Each team has various cheer songs and cheering methods, so you can enjoy the baseball stadium atmosphere even if you don't know much about baseball. You can also enjoy delicious food while watching the game. Particularly popular is '치맥(치킨과 맥주)'(chicken and beer). If you're curious about Korean cheering culture, definitely visit a Korean baseball game.

▸ **각 단어와 한글을 연결해 보세요.** Match each word to the correct Korean.

축구 ·   · taekwondo

농구 ·   · swimming

야구 ·   · tennis

스키 ·   · badminton

배드민턴 ·   · baseball

테니스 ·   · basketball

수영 ·   · skiing

태권도 ·   · soccer

볼링 ·   · bowling

▸ NCT 운동 Report NCT Sports Match-Up

What are the favorite sports of NCT members? Write them in the space below.

Nct Exercise Report

NAME	
재민	
EXERCISE	
배드민턴	

NAME
양양
EXERCISE

NAME
샤오쥔
EXERCISE

NAME
마크
EXERCISE

NAME
천러
EXERCISE

NAME
제노
EXERCISE

NAME
지성
EXERCISE

NAME
헨드리
EXERCISE

NAME
정우
EXERCISE

NAME
해찬
EXERCISE

CHAPTER 3

NCT's SOCIAL LIFE

그전에 출석 체크 한번 부르자.

[geu-jeon-e chul-sseok che-keu han-beon bu-reu-ja]

Before that, let's call attendance.

Let's learn some words related to school. Trace the words and freely practice in the blank spaces.

수업
[su-eop]
class

수업

숙제
[suk-jje]
homework

숙제

출석
[chul-sseok]
attendance

출석

지각하다
[ji-ga-ka-da]
be late

지각하다

입학하다
[i-pa-ka-da]
enroll

입학하다

교복
[gyo-bok]
school uniform

교복

반장
[ban-jang]
class leader

반장

교무실
[gyo-mu-sil]
teacher's office

교무실

급식
[geup-ssik]
school meal

급식

Practice words

대학교에 입학했어요.
I entered university.

수업이 너무 많아요.
I have too many classes.

숙제 있어?
Do you have any homework?

오늘 지각했어.
I was late today.

In Korean middle and high schools, students wear designated '교복' according to school rules. Lunch is provided as 급식. The daily varying menu of school meals is very important to students. Since each school has different meals, students often compare school lunches between schools. Some schools occasionally serve special meals like lobster.

▶ 각 단어와 한글을 연결해 보세요. Match each word to the correct Korean.

수업 •   • school meal

출석 •   • school uniform

지각하다 •   • class leader

숙제 •   • attendance

입학하다 •   • be late

반장 •   • teacher's office

교복 •   • class

교무실 •   • homework

급식 •   • enroll

If the members go to school, what roles would suit them? Match each member to a suitable role.

교장
principal

sticker

교감
vice principal

sticker

담임
homeroom teacher

sticker

반장
class leader

sticker

체육부장
athletic director

sticker

청소부장
class cleaning director

sticker

봉사부장
service coordinator

sticker

총무
administrative director

sticker

도서부장
library director

sticker

도영   너랑 밥을 제일 많이 먹고 싶어 하지 나는

Check through video

선생님이 얘기하셨어, 선생님이.

[seon-saeng-ni-mi yae-gi-ha-syeo-sseo, seon-saeng-ni-mi]

NCT Korean Vocabulary note

The makeup artist said that.

Let's learn about occupations. Trace the words and freely practice in the blank spaces.

	학생 [hak-ssaeng] student	학생
	선생님 [seon-saeng-nim] teacher	선생님
	회사원 [hoe-sa-won] office worker	회사원
	의사 [ui-sa] doctor	의사
	간호사 [gan-ho-sa] nurse	간호사
	경찰 [gyeong-chal] police officer	경찰
	소방관 [so-bang-gwan] firefighter	소방관
	운동선수 [un-dong-seon-su] athlete	운동선수
	요리사 [yo-ri-sa] chef	요리사

Practice words

> 회사원**이에요?**
> Are you an office worker?

> 저는 학생**이에요.**
> I am a student.

> 소방관**이 꿈이야.**
> My dream is to be a firefighter.

> 나중에 요리사**가 될 거야.**
> I want to become a chef in the future.

When asking about someone's occupation, ask "무슨 일해요?"(What do you do?) or "직업이 뭐예요?"(What's your job?). When answering such questions, respond with "N 이에요/예요"(It is N). Use '-이에요' for nouns with a final consonant and '-예요' for nouns without a final consonant.

Example: No final consonant: 요리사 ➜ 요리사예요, With final consonant: 경찰 ➜ 경찰이에요 *받침(final consonant)

▸ **각 단어와 한글을 연결해 보세요.** Match each word to the correct Korean.

학생 •   • doctor

선생님 •   • chef

회사원 •   • nurse

의사 •   • police officer

간호사 •   • teacher

경찰 •   • athlete

소방관 •   • student

운동선수 •   • firefighter

요리사 •   • office worker

104

If NCT members weren't singers, what jobs would suit them? Place each member's sticker next to a suitable job.

경찰 →

운동선수 →

선생님 →

의사 →

소방관 →

간호사 →

요리사 →

회사원 →

NCT's KOREAN VOCABULARY NOTE

TAEYONG | 저희 NCT 127이

Check through video

영상 편지 보내겠습니다.

[yeong-sang pyeon-ji bo-nae-get-seum-ni-da]

I'll send her a video letter.

NCT Korean Vocabulary note

Learn some words related to Social Media. Trace the words and freely practice in the blank spaces.

보내다

[bo-nae-da]
send

보내다

받다

[bat-tta]
receive

받다

공유하다

[gong-yu-ha-da]
share

공유하다

올리다

[ol-li-da]
upload

올리다

쓰다

[sseu-da]
write

쓰다

댓글

[dae-kkeul]
comment

댓글

저장하다

[jeo-jang-ha-da]
save

저장하다

추가하다

[chu-ga-ha-da]
add

추가하다

누르다

[nu-reu-da]
press

누르다

Practice words

사진 저장했어요.
I saved the photo.

댓글 달았어요.
I left a comment.

인스타그램에 올렸어.
I posted it on Instagram.

메시지 보냈어.
I sent a message.

When writing on Social Media, people add '#' followed by keywords at the end of posts. The '#' is read as '해시태그[haesitaegeu]'(hashtag) or sometimes '샵[syap]'(sharp).

▸ **각 단어와 한글을 연결해 보세요.** Match each word to the correct Korean.

받다 •　　　　　　　• comment

공유하다 •　　　　　　• receive

올리다 •　　　　　　　• save

보내다 •　　　　　　　• add

댓글 •　　　　　　　　• send

저장하다 •　　　　　　• write

누르다 •　　　　　　　• share

추가하다 •　　　　　　• press

쓰다 •　　　　　　　　• upload

▸ NCT 멤버들과 일상 공유하기 Daily Sharing

Write down NCTzens' daily routine in the blank space below.

친구에게 DM 보내기.
Sending a DM to a friend.

멋있는 사진 올리기.
Posting a cool photo.

시즈니에게 소식 전하기.
Sharing news with NCTzens.

NCT 영상 보기.
Watching NCT videos.

Check through video

지금 데이트 신청한 거야?

[ji-geum de-i-teu sin-cheong-han geo-ya?]

Are you asking me out?

Learn some words related to dating. Trace the words and freely practice in the blank spaces.

데이트
[de-i-teu]
date

데이트

소개팅
[so-gae-ting]
blind date

소개팅

미팅
[mi-ting]
group blind date

미팅

사귀다
[sa-gwi-da]
be in a relationship

사귀다

좋아하다
[jo-a-ha-da]
like

좋아하다

여자 친구
[yeo-ja chin-gu]
girlfriend

여자 친구

남자 친구
[nam-ja chin-gu]
boyfriend

남자 친구

헤어지다
[he-eo-ji-da]
break up

헤어지다

사랑하다
[sa-rang-ha-da]
love

사랑하다

Practice words

시즈니 사랑해요!
I love you, NCTzens!

많이 좋아해요.
I like you a lot.

내일 데이트하러 가.
I'm going on a date tomorrow.

오늘부터 사귀기로 했어.
We decided to go out from today.

In Korea, there is a culture of celebrating anniversaries when dating. They celebrate anniversaries every 100 days, such as the 100일(100th day), 200일(200th day), etc. On these anniversaries, they exchange gifts and celebrate by eating at romantic places.

▶ **각 단어와 한글을 연결해 보세요.** Match each word to the correct Korean.

사랑하다 •	• like
여자 친구 •	• boyfriend
남자 친구 •	• group blind date
좋아하다 •	• be in a relationship
미팅 •	• love
사귀다 •	• date
데이트 •	• girlfriend
소개팅 •	• break up
헤어지다 •	• blind date

TO THE WORLD.

여기는 NCT!

안녕하세요, NCT 입니다.

TO THE WORLD.

여기는 NCT!

안녕하세요, NCT 입니다.

Practice writing the greeting.

⑤ 친구 chin-gu

Check through video

우리 둘이 처음 만났을 때 생각나요?

[u-ri du-ri cheo-eum man-na-sseul ttae saeng-gang-na-yo?]

NCT Korean Vocabulary note

Do you remember when we first met?

Let's learn words related to friendship. Trace the words and freely practice in the blank spaces.

	놀다 [nol-da] play	놀다
	만나다 [man-na-da] meet	만나다
	우정 [u-jeong] friendship	우정
	싸우다 [ssa-u-da] fight	싸우다
	화해하다 [hwa-hae-ha-da] reconcile	화해하다
	데려오다 [de-ryeo-o-da] bring along	데려오다
	부르다 [bu-reu-da] call	부르다
	친하다 [chin-ha-da] be close	친하다
	소중하다 [so-jung-ha-da] cherish	소중하다

Practice words

소중한 제 친구예요.
This is my cherished friend.

집에서 같이 놀았어요.
We hung out together at home.

친하게 지내자.
Let's be close friends.

학교 앞에서 만나.
Let's meet in front of the school.

If you want to become friends with someone, try saying '친하게 지내자', Friends of similar age can become close with just this simple phrase. When introducing a friend, say '제 친구 N이에요/예요'(This is my friend N). Insert the friend's name in place of N when introducing them.

▸ **각 단어와 한글을 연결해 보세요.** Match each word to the correct Korean.

놀다 •	• friendship
만나다 •	• fight
우정 •	• cherish
싸우다 •	• be close
부르다 •	• play
친하다 •	• meet
소중하다 •	• call
화해하다 •	• bring along
데려오다 •	• reconcile

Find the words below hidden in the puzzle.

보기

놀다	만나다	우정	소중하다
화해하다	싸우다	부르다	친하다

지	금	우	리	함	께	노	래	해	요
놀	면	추	우	리	의	말	만	나	다
다	정	억	정	성	스	러	운	음	즐
지	금	의	나	에	게	소	나	기	거
공	기	만	두	려	운	중	서	로	운
너	와	남	이	떨	림	하	조	명	화
싸	우	다	가	부	르	다	웃	음	해
내	일	어	제	친	구	와	소	풍	하
모	두	친	하	다	이	간	편	하	다
좋	다	구	서	로	가	좋	은	이	웃

Check through video

맛있다.

[ma-sit-tta]

It's so delicious.

NCT Korean Vocabulary note

Let's learn taste vocabulary. Trace the words and freely practice in the blank spaces.

	달다 [dal-da] sweet	달다
	짜다 [jja-da] salty	짜다
	맵다 [maep-tta] spicy	맵다
	시다 [si-da] sour	시다
	싱겁다 [sing-geop-tta] not salty enough	싱겁다
	쓰다 [sseu-da] bitter	쓰다
	고소하다 [go-so-ha-da] nutty	고소하다
	맛있다 [ma-sit-tta] delicious	맛있다
	맛없다 [ma-deop-tta] tasteless	맛없다

Practice
words

아이스크림이 **달아요.**
The ice cream is sweet.

김치찌개가 **짜요.**
The kimchi stew is salty.

떡볶이가 정말 **매워요.**
The tteokbokki is really spicy.

국이 너무 **싱거워요.**
This soup is not salty enough.

Do you know '단짠단짠[danjjandanjjan]'? '단짠단짠' is a modern Korean slang that combines '달다'(sweet) and '짜다'(salty) in repetition. It's used when a food alternates between sweet and salty tastes. Typical examples include 'tteokbokki,' 'Korean fried chicken,' 'caramel popcorn,' and 'bulgogi.' The term '단짠단짠' can also describe the enjoyment of eating multiple dishes with contrasting flavors in one meal.

▸ **각 단어와 한글을 연결해 보세요.** Match each word to the correct Korean.

맛없다 •   • delicious

시다 •   • bitter

달다 •   • salty

맛있다 •   • sweet

쓰다 •   • sour

고소하다 •   • tasteless

맵다 •   • spicy

싱겁다 •   • nutty

짜다 •   • not salty enough

Find the Korean words using these consonants, then write their English meanings.

 **sweet**

 spicy

 **salty**

 **sour**

 **bitter**

NCT's KOREAN VOCABULARY NOTE

Check through video

<u>선배</u>님!

[seon-bae-nim!]

NCT Korean Vocabulary note

<u>Sir!</u>

▸ 새로운 단어 배우기 New Words

Let's learn words related to social life. Trace the words and freely practice in the blank spaces.

입사 [ip-ssa] join a company	입사
선배 [seon-bae] senior	선배
후배 [hu-bae] junior	후배
회식 [hoe-sik] work dinner	회식
퇴근하다 [toe-geun-ha-da] get off work	퇴근하다
아르바이트 [a-reu-ba-i-teu] part time job	아르바이트
월급 [wol-geup] momthly salary	월급
회사 [hoe-sa] company	회사
출근 [chul-geun] go to work	출근

Practice words

SM 회사 선배님들이세요.
These are seniors from SM Entertainment.

**첫 월급 받았어요?
축하해요.**
Did you get your first salary?
Congratulations.

**후배님, 신곡 댄스
챌린지 함께해요.**
Hey junior, let's do the dance
challenge for the new song together.

**SM에 입사하려면
어떻게 해야 하나요?**
How do I join SM Entertainment?

How do you address people in a company? Add '○○ 님' after names or titles, or
'○○ 씨' after names. For names, use '도영 님, 도영 씨,' and for positions or titles,
use '팀장님, 선배님'(Team Leader-nim, Senior-nim).

▸ **각 단어와 한글을 연결해 보세요.** Match each word to the correct Korean.

입사 •   • go to work

선배 •   • company

후배 •   • work dinner

회식 •   • join a company

퇴근하다 •   • part time job

아르바이트 •   • get off work

월급 •   • senior

회사 •   • junior

출근 •   • monthly salary

How can I become an SM trainee like NCT? Write your preferred senior's name in parentheses.

외국인 시즈니

저는 SM의 연습생이 되고 싶은 외국인이에요.
어떤 준비가 필요할까요?
I'm a foreigner interested in becoming an SM trainee.
What should I do to prepare?

NCT 선배(   )

안녕하세요. 반가워요.
제 생각에는 연습이 제일 중요한 것 같아요.
Hello. It's nice to meet you. I think practicing is the most important part.

외국인 시즈니

노래와 춤, 무엇을 연습해야 할까요?
What should I focus on, singing or dancing?

NCT 선배(   )

둘 다 중요해요.
그리고 한국어 공부도 중요해요.
Both are important. And studying Korean is also essential.

외국인 시즈니

《NCT's KOREAN VOCABULARY NOTE》로
공부하고 있어요.
I'm studying with
《NCT's KOREAN VOCABULARY NOTE》.

NCT 선배(   )

저도 봤어요. 좋은 책이에요. 열심히 공부해서 SM에서 만나요!
I've seen it too. It's a great book. Study hard, and I hope to see you at SM!

색 saek

Check through video

저는 노란색 좋아해요.

[jeo-neun no-ran-saek jo-a-hae-yo]

I like yellow.

NCT
Korean
Vocabulary
note

Let's learn color vocabulary. Trace the words and freely practice in the blank spaces.

흰색
[hin-saek]
white

검은색
[geo-meun-saek]
black

초록색
[cho-rok-ssaek]
green

노란색
[no-ran-saek]
yellow

빨간색
[ppal-gan-saek]
red

파란색
[pa-ran-saek]
blue

주황색
[ju-hwang-saek]
orange

분홍색
[bun-hong-saek]
pink

보라색
[bo-ra-saek]
purple

Practice words

▶ **주요 표현을 배워 보세요.** Learn key expressions.

재민은 흰 셔츠가
잘 어울려요.
JAEMIN looks good with a white shirt.

태용이 형이 초록색으로
머리를 염색했어.
TAEYONG dyed his hair green.

마크, 주황색 모자
어디서 샀어?
MARK, where did you buy
the orange hat?

해찬이 잠옷은 검은색이야.
HAECHAN's pajamas are black.

'어울리다' is a Korean verb that describes when people get along well or when objects harmonize well together. This word can be translated into English as 'to match,' 'to suit,' or 'looks good.' For example, if two people get along well, they might be good friends or partners.

▶ **각 단어와 한글을 연결해 보세요.** Match each word to the correct Korean.

보라색 •	• blue
빨간색 •	• purple
초록색 •	• white
분홍색 •	• black
흰색 •	• red
검은색 •	• yellow
주황색 •	• green
노란색 •	• pink
파란색 •	• orange

▸ NCT 머리카락 색 매칭 Report NCT Hair Color Match-Up

Which hair colors would suit NCT members?

런쥔

제노

재민

색 ----------------- ----------------- -----------------

천러

쟈니

헨드리

색 ----------------- ----------------- -----------------

해찬

쿤

양양

색 ----------------- ----------------- -----------------

Check through video

귀엽다, 뭘 해도 귀여운 거.

[gwi-yeop-tta, mwol hae-do gwi-yeo-un geo]

Whatever I do, people always say, "Oh, so cute."

Let's learn appearance vocabulary. Trace the words and freely practice in the blank spaces.

예쁘다
[ye-ppeu-da]
pretty

예쁘다

귀엽다
[gwi-yeop-tta]
cute

귀엽다

잘생기다
[jal-saeng-gi-da]
handsome

잘생기다

못생기다
[mot-ssaeng-gi-da]
ugly

못생기다

크다
[keu-da]
big

크다

아름답다
[a-reum-dap-tta]
beautiful

아름답다

작다
[jak-tta]
small

작다

날씬하다
[nal-ssin-ha-da]
slim

날씬하다

뚱뚱하다
[ttung-ttung-ha-da]
overweight

뚱뚱하다

Practice
words

오늘 마크 형 진짜 잘생겼는데?
Mark looks really handsome today, doesn't he?

서울 야경 정말 아름답다.
Seoul's night view is truly beautiful.

강아지가 정말 귀여워요.
The puppy is really cute.

제 방은 조금 작아요.
My room is a bit small.

There's a word '동안' in Korean. It refers to people who look younger than their actual age. People say "정말 동안이세요"(You look so young) or "진짜 동안이다"(You really look young) to such people. Conversely, '노안' refers to people who look older than their actual age. However, this word isn't complimentary, so it's better not to use it.

▸ **각 단어와 한글을 연결해 보세요.** Match each word to the correct Korean.

뚱뚱하다 •   • big

잘생기다 •   • cute

예쁘다 •   • ugly

귀엽다 •   • small

작다 •   • beautiful

날씬하다 •   • overweight

못생기다 •   • handsome

크다 •   • slim

아름답다 •   • pretty

퍼스널 컬러

Personal color

Personal color refers to colors that best match an individual's skin tone, eye color, and hair color. Everyone has their own unique colors, and choosing complementary colors for clothing, hair, and makeup can enhance one's complexion, making their face look brighter and more vibrant. Personal colors are typically divided into four types: Spring, Summer, Fall, and Winter, each associated with a unique set of colors. Many Koreans often consult experts for personal color analysis and use this information to choose clothes and cosmetics that suit them.

| Spring type | Summer type | Fall type | Winter type |

- Spring type: Warm and bright colors (light beige, bright yellow)

- Summer type: Cool and soft colors (pastel tones, light pink)

- Fall type: Warm and deep colors (camel, olive, brown)

- Winter type: Cool and clear colors (black, cool tone blue, pure white)

Check
through
video

항상 그 아메리카노 벤티 사이즈 하고.

[hang-sang geu a-me-ri-ka-no ben-ti sa-i-jeu ha-go]

She always orders americano
in venti size.

NCT
Korean
Vocabulary
note

Let's learn words related to shopping. Trace the words and freely practice in the blank spaces.

쇼핑하다
[syo-ping-ha-da]
to shop

쇼핑하다

사다
[sa-da]
to buy

사다

싸다
[ssa-da]
cheap

싸다

가격
[ga-gyeok]
price

가격

비싸다
[bi-ssa-da]
expensive

비싸다

교환하다
[gyo-hwan-ha-da]
to exchange

교환하다

사이즈
[sa-i-jeu]
size

사이즈

포장하다
[po-jang-ha-da]
to wrap

포장하다

깎다
[kkak-tta]
discount

깎다

Practice words

뭐 샀어요?
What did you buy?

주로 어디에서 쇼핑해요?
Where do you usually shop?

사이즈가 좀 큰 것 같아요.
The size seems a bit big.

사장님, 조금만 깎아 주세요.
Please, give me a little discount.

When describing '깎다[kkakda]' in the context of reducing the price of an item, it refers to the act of lowering the price demanded by the seller during price negotiations. It is commonly used when buyers propose a lower price at markets or stores. In English, it can be expressed as "to bargain", "to negotiate the price", or "discount". This term is typically used in informal settings or where price tags are not fixed.

▸ 각 단어와 한글을 연결해 보세요. Match each word to the correct Korean.

쇼핑하다 •	• to wrap
싸다 •	• expensive
사다 •	• cheap
가격 •	• discount
비싸다 •	• size
교환하다 •	• to buy
사이즈 •	• price
깎다 •	• to exchange
포장하다 •	• to shop

성수동

Hot Place Seongsu-dong

Let me introduce Seongsu-dong, a trendy spot popular among foreign visitors to Korea. It features various pop-up and flagship stores showcasing beauty and fashion brands, making it popular not only among the domestic Millennials and Generation Z but also with foreigners.

Foreign visitors come here to experience and purchase well-known brands they've seen on social media, as well as products available only in Korea. The area is also filled with unique cafes and distinctive shops, creating a stylish street vibe.

Moreover, as SM Entertainment's headquarters is located in Seongsu-dong, it's a must-visit for K-pop fans worldwide. At the KWANGYA Store, you can find albums and various merchandise from SM Entertainment artists.

KWANGYA Store Location: B1, D Tower Prest, Exit 4, Seoul Forest Station on the Suin-Bundang Line

CHAPTER 4

NCT's
SPACE

Check through video

이태용 혹시 뭐 후렴구가 있어? 멜로디나?

거울은 거짓말하지 않는다.

[geo-u-leun geo-jin-mal-ha-ji an-neun-da]

NCT Korean Vocabulary note

A mirror does not lie.

Let's learn names of household items. Trace the words and freely practice in the blank spaces.

소파
[so-pa]
sofa

소파 _____

텔레비전
[te-le-bi-jeon]
television

텔레비전 _____

거울
[geo-ul]
mirror

거울 _____

옷장
[ot-jjang]
wardrobe

옷장 _____

에어컨
[e-eo-keon]
air conditioner

에어컨 _____

침대
[chim-dae]
bed

침대 _____

식탁
[sik-tak]
dining table

식탁 _____

책장
[chaek-jjang]
bookshelf

책장 _____

선풍기
[seon-pung-gi]
fan

선풍기 _____

Practice words

▸ **주요 표현을 배워 보세요.** Learn key expressions.

침대에 눕자마자 잠들었어요.
I fell asleep as soon as I got in bed.

소파에 앉아서 TV를 봐요.
I watch TV sitting on the sofa.

옷장에 옷이 별로 없어요.
There aren't many clothes in the wardrobe.

에어컨 좀 켜 주세요.
Please turn on the air conditioner.

Korea has various types of housing. There are '아파트'(apartments), '빌라'(villas), '단독주택'(single-family homes), and '오피스텔'(officetels). 아파트 are the most common form of housing in Korea, while 빌라 are multi-family houses with 2-5 floors. 단독주택 often have yards and more private space. 오피스텔 is a combination of '오피스'(office) and '호텔'(hotel), combining residential and office functions.

▸ **각 단어와 한글을 연결해 보세요.** Match each word to the correct Korean.

거울 •   • television

소파 •   • bed

옷장 •   • dining table

식탁 •   • fan

텔레비전 •   • sofa

선풍기 •   • mirror

책장 •   • air conditioner

에어컨 •   • wardrobe

침대 •   • bookshelf

Find the words below hidden in the puzzle.

보기

| 에어컨 | 거울 | 침대 | 선풍기 |
| 옷장 | 식탁 | 텔레비전 | 소파 | 책장 |

컴	퓨	터	거	실	조	명	침	신	발
양	털	소	파	사	이	불	대	액	자
탄	양	의	자	진	저	선	담	그	림
자	말	거	울	첩	보	풍	요	명	화
시	계	매	트	리	스	기	스	탠	드
러	소	에	어	컨	전	구	식	탁	꽃
그	설	곰	인	형	텔	라	디	오	병
정	책	장	서	랍	레	옷	선	옷	화
리	상	바	구	니	비	걸	반	장	분
장	난	감	상	자	전	이	슬	리	퍼

그 회의실 좀 체크해 봐.

[gue hoe-ui-sil jom che-keu-hae bwa]

Go check the conference room.

▸ 새로운 단어 배우기 New Words

Let's learn some words related to the office. Trace the words and freely practice in the blank spaces.

	복사기 [bok-ssa-gi] photocopier	복사기
	명함 [myeong-ham] business card	명함
	서류 [seo-ryu] document	서류
	회의실 [hoe-ui-sil] conference room	회의실
	컴퓨터 [keom-pyu-teo] computer	컴퓨터
	서랍 [seo-rap] drawer	서랍
	도장 [do-jang] stamp	도장
	슬리퍼 [seul-li-peo] slippers	슬리퍼
	전화기 [jeon-hwa-gi] telephone	전화기

Practice words

▸ 주요 표현을 배워 보세요. Learn key expressions.

이건 제 명함이에요.
This is my business card.

회의실 제가 예약했어요.
I reserved the meeting room.

도장이 필요해요.
어디에 있어요?
I need a seal. Where is it?

서류에 사인해 주세요.
Please sign the document.

While the importance of 명함(business card) varies by country, it's generally customary in Korea to exchange business cards when meeting employees from other companies. Business cards include name, company name, position, email, phone number, and company address.

▸ 각 단어와 한글을 연결해 보세요. Match each word to the correct Korean.

복사기 •   • computer

명함 •   • slippers

서류 •   • drawer

회의실 •   • telephone

서랍 •   • photocopier

도장 •   • business card

슬리퍼 •   • stamp

전화기 •   • conference room

컴퓨터 •   • document

Match the words to the verbs and write down the sentences below.

편지
letter

사용하다
to use

명함
business card

받다
receive

펜
pen

쓰다
to write

컴퓨터
computer

내려받다
download

민초 샴푸 있어.

[min-cho syam-pu it-sseo]

I have mint chocolate

shampoo too.

Let's learn bathroom vocabulary. Trace the words and freely practice in the blank spaces.

shampoo	**샴푸** [syam-pu] shampoo	샴푸
	린스 [rin-seu] hair conditioner	린스
	세면대 [se-myeon-dae] sink	세면대
	수건 [su-geon] towel	수건
	칫솔 [chi-ssol] toothbrush	칫솔
	치약 [chi-yak] toothpaste	치약
	비누 [bi-nu] soap	비누
	욕조 [yok-jjo] bathtub	욕조
	샤워 [sya-wo] shower	샤워

Practice words

샴푸가 다 떨어졌어.
The shampoo is all gone.

수건 좀 바꿔 주세요.
Please change the towel.

치약 다 썼어.
I used up all the toothpaste.

저는 보통 샤워하면서
스트레스를 풀어요.
I usually relieve stress while showering.

'샤워하다' can also be expressed as '목욕하다' or '씻다'. '씻다' is mainly used with body parts like hands and feet, as in '손을 씻다'(wash hands) or '발을 씻다'(wash feet), while for face, '세수하다'(wash up) is commonly used. For washing hair, the expression '머리를 감다'(wash one's hair) is used.

▸ **각 단어와 한글을 연결해 보세요.** Match each word to the correct Korean.

샴푸 •	• shower
린스 •	• soap
세면대 •	• bathtub
수건 •	• shampoo
칫솔 •	• hair conditioner
치약 •	• towel
비누 •	• toothbrush
욕조 •	• toothpaste
샤워 •	• sink

▸ 한글 미로 Korean Maze

Help JUNGWOO find his way to XIAOJUN. Follow the pictures that contain the letter '人' to find the way.

배달 음식 너무 많이 먹으니까

[bae-dal eum-sik neo-mu ma-ni meo-geu-ni-kka]

It's just I eat too much delivery food.

Let's learn restaurant vocabulary. Trace the words and freely practice in the blank spaces.

	숟가락 [sut-kka-rak] spoon	숟가락
	젓가락 [jeo-kka-rak] chopstick	젓가락
	메뉴 [me-nyu] menu	메뉴
	컵 [keop] cup	컵
	그릇 [geu-reut] bowl	그릇
	접시 [jeop-si] plate	접시
	음료수 [eum-nyo-su] drink	음료수
	음식 [eum-sik] food	음식
	반찬 [ban-chan] side dish	반찬

Practice words

사장님, 반찬 좀 더 주세요.
Could we have some more side dishes, please?

음료수 하나 더 시킬까?
Shall we order another drink?

이 식당 음식이 정말 맛있다.
The food at this restaurant is really delicious.

사장님, 메뉴판 좀 주세요.
Please give us a menu.

In Korea, you can have various foods delivered. Chicken delivery is especially popular among Koreans. You can order through mobile delivery applications and receive food within 30 minutes to 1 hour after placing your order. Since tipping culture isn't common in Korea, you don't need to tip delivery drivers separately.

▶ **각 단어와 한글을 연결해 보세요.** Match each word to the correct Korean.

음료수 ·   · menu

숟가락 ·   · cup

젓가락 ·   · bowl

접시 ·   · spoon

그릇 ·   · chopstick

음식 ·   · food

메뉴 ·   · drink

반찬 ·   · plate

컵 ·   · side dish

키오스크

KIOSK

In Korea, you can easily find self-ordering kiosks at restaurants. While you might expect to order from machines at the front of the store, technology has advanced, and now small kiosks are attached to each table, allowing customers to order and pay directly from their seats.

These kiosks also have buttons for calling staff and requesting water, napkins, etc., removing the need to call staff directly. Language options are also available, making it easy to use for those who aren't fluent in Korean.

Table-attached kiosks are commonly used in restaurants, while cafes and burger chains usually place larger kiosks at the entrance.

종이는 있어, 종이, 펜.

[jong-i-neun it-sseo, jong-i, pen]

I have a paper and a pen.

Let's learn stationery vocabulary. Trace the words and freely practice in the blank spaces.

	연필 [yeon-pil] pencil	연필
	볼펜/펜 [bol-pen] ballpoint pen	볼펜
	지우개 [ji-u-gae] eraser	지우개
	자 [ja] ruler	자
	메모지 [me-mo-ji] memo pad	메모지
	책 [chaek] book	책
	필통 [pil-tong] pencil case	필통
	풀 [pul] glue	풀
	색연필 [saeng-nyeon-pil] colored pencil	색연필

 Practice words

지우개 **누구 거야?**
Whose eraser is this?

필통 **누구 거야?**
Whose pencil case is this?

연필 **말고 볼펜으로 써.**
Write with a ballpoint pen, not a pencil.

책 **말고 공책에 적어.**
Write it in a notebook, not a book.

'적다[jeokda]' and '쓰다[sseuda]' have similar meanings in Korean, but there are slight differences. '적다' is mainly used to indicate the act of writing characters when composing words or sentences. On the other hand, '쓰다' encompasses not only the act of writing characters but also the act of writing or drawing on various objects or surfaces.

▸ **각 단어와 한글을 연결해 보세요.** Match each word to the correct Korean.

연필 •   • colored pencil

볼펜/펜 •   • glue

지우개 •   • pencil case

자 •   • pencil

메모지 •   • ballpoint pen

책 •   • eraser

필통 •   • ruler

풀 •   • memo pad

색연필 •   • book

▶ **숨은 낱말 찾기** Finding Hidden Words

Find the words below hidden in the puzzle.

보기

연필	볼펜	필통	자
지우개	책	풀	메모지

텔	레	비	전	정	컴	퓨	터	이	금
연	필	집	지	우	개	마	크	상	식
애	통	엔	시	티	문	구	점	한	먹
도	장	고	등	학	교	책	우	표	기
명	함	공	부	교	실	랑	슬	리	퍼
한	글	날	교	장	선	생	님	아	우
글	자	강	아	지	풀	반	장	이	산
공	책	산	글	쓰	기	베	이	스	볼
무	읽	에	메	모	지	볼	펜	크	림
원	기	필	기	도	구	준	비	림	장

재민 | 지금 전 컬러 렌즈도 꼈구용

지금 저는 컬러렌즈도 꼈고요.

[ji-geum jeo-neun keol-leo-len-jeu-do kkyeot-go-yo]

I have colored contacts on.

NCT Korean Vocabulary note

Let's learn some words related to apparel. Trace these words and practice writing them in the blank spaces.

치마

[chi-ma]
skirt

치마

바지

[ba-ji]
pants

바지

티셔츠

[ti-syeo-cheu]
T-shirt

티셔츠

양말

[yang-mal]
socks

양말

구두

[gu-du]
shoes

구두

운동화

[un-dong-hwa]
sneakers

운동화

옷

[ot]
clothes

옷

안경

[an-gyeong]
glasses

안경

렌즈

[ren-jeu]
contact lenses

렌즈

Practice
words

이 옷 한번 입어 보세요.
Please try on these clothes.

지성이가 선물해 준 바지예요.
These are the pants JISUNG gave me as a gift.

안경을 쓰니까 분위기가 다르다.
You look different with glasses on.

운동화를 신으니까 발이 편하다.
These sneakers are comfortable on my feet.

The verbs '입다'(wear), '신다'(put on), '쓰다'(wear), '끼다'(put on) are used differently depending on the noun that precedes them. Clothes like skirts and pants use '입다', shoes and socks use '신다', glasses and hats use '쓰다', and rings and contact lenses use '끼다'.

▸ **각 단어와 한글을 연결해 보세요.** Match each word to the correct Korean.

치마 •   • contact lenses

바지 •   • glasses

티셔츠 •   • clothes

양말 •   • sneakers

구두 •   • skirt

운동화 •   • pants

옷 •   • T-shirt

안경 •   • shoes

렌즈 •   • socks

Look at the picture and the initial consonants, then guess the word.

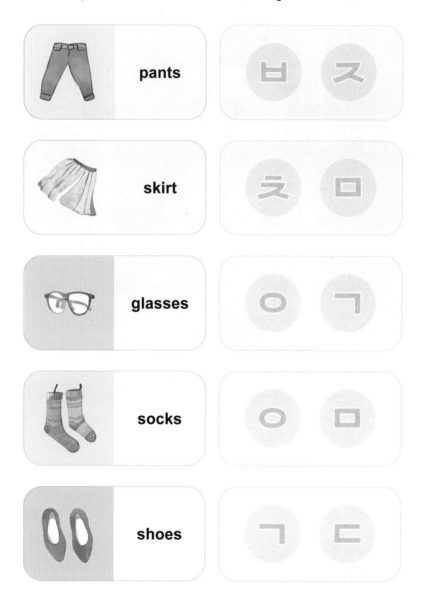

NCT's KOREAN VOCABULARY NOTE

Check through video

어, 좋은데요? 모자?

[eo, jo-eun-de-yo? mo-ja?]

Wow, I like that. The hat?

NCT Korean Vocabulary note

Let's learn some words related to fashion. Trace these words and practice writing them in the blank spaces.

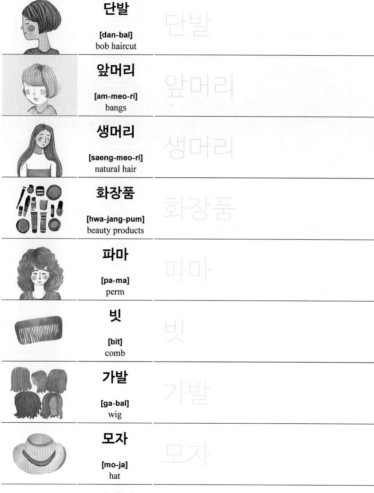

	단발 [dan-bal] bob haircut	단발
	앞머리 [am-meo-ri] bangs	앞머리
	생머리 [saeng-meo-ri] natural hair	생머리
	화장품 [hwa-jang-pum] beauty products	화장품
	파마 [pa-ma] perm	파마
	빗 [bit] comb	빗
	가발 [ga-bal] wig	가발
	모자 [mo-ja] hat	모자
	머리핀 [meo-ri-pin] hairpin	머리핀

Practice words

저 **단발**머리 잘 어울리나요?
Does this bob cut suit me well?

앞머리를 자르고
싶어요.
I want to cut my bangs.

가발을 써서
못 알아봤어요.
I couldn't recognize you because
you were wearing a wig.

어제 미용실에서
파마했어.
I got a perm at the hair salon
yesterday.

What should you say when going to a hair salon in Korea? Use '-고 싶어요'(I want to): '머리를 자르고 싶어요'(I want to cut my hair), '파마를 하고 싶어요'(I want to get a perm), '염색을 하고 싶어요'(I want to dye my hair).
And use '-아/어 주세요'(Please verbs). '머리를 조금만 잘라 주세요'(Please cut my hair a little), '이렇게 파마해 주세요'(Please perm it like this), '분홍색으로 염색해 주세요'(Please dye it pink).

▸ **각 단어와 한글을 연결해 보세요.** Match each word to the correct Korean.

단발 •   • hairpin

앞머리 •   • hat

생머리 •   • wig

화장품 •   • comb

파마 •   • bob haircut

빗 •   • bangs

가발 •   • natural hair

모자 •   • beauty products

머리핀 •   • perm

Learn conversation you have at hair salon.

헤어샵   어서 오세요. 어떻게 해 드릴까요?
Welcome, how can I help you today?

정우   커트를 하고 싶어요.
아, 쟈니 형, 머리할 거죠?
I'd like a haircut. Ah, JOHNNY, you're getting your hair done, right?

쟈니   나는 염색하고 싶어.
I want to dye my hair.

정우   커트보다 염색이 오래 걸리니까 형 먼저 해요.
Dyeing takes longer than a haircut, so you go first.

쟈니   오, 고마워.
Oh, thanks.

헤어샵   그럼 한 분은 음료를 드시면서 기다려 주세요.
Then, one of you can enjoy a drink while you wait.

Check through video

도영   가위 여기 있어

가위 **여기 있어.**

[ga-wi yeo-gi it-sseo]

NCT Korean Vocabulary note

I found the scissors.

Let's learn the names of kitchen utensils. Trace the words and practice writing them in the blank spaces.

가스레인지

[ga-seu-re-in-ji]
gas range

가스레인지

프라이팬

[peu-ra-i-paen]
frying pan

프라이팬

냄비

[naem-bi]
pot

냄비

가위

[ga-wi]
scissors

가위

전자레인지

[jeon-ja-re-in-ji]
microwave

전자레인지

밥솥

[bap-ssot]
rice cooker

밥솥

칼

[kal]
knife

칼

국자

[guk-jja]
ladle

국자

도마

[do-ma]
cutting board

도마

Practice words

▶ **주요 표현을 배워 보세요.** Learn key expressions.

가스레인지 불 껐어?
Did you turn off the gas stove?

전자레인지에 넣고 5분 돌려.
Put it in the microwave for 5 minutes.

칼로 채소를 먼저 썰자.
Let's cut the vegetables
with a knife first.

밥솥에 밥이 있어.
There's rice in the rice cooker.

Gas ranges have letters for '약'(weak), '중'(medium), and '강'(strong) written on them. These indicate flame intensity. They're abbreviated forms of '약불(weak heat), 중불(medium heat), 강불(strong heat)'. When asking to adjust the flame, say things like "불 좀 줄여 주세요"(Please lower the heat), "불 좀 약하게 해 주세요"(Please make it lower), "불 좀 세게 해 주세요"(Please make it stronger), "강불로 해 주세요"(Please set it to high heat).

▶ **각 단어와 한글을 연결해 보세요.** Match each word to the correct Korean.

가스레인지 •   • ladle

프라이팬 •   • microwave

냄비 •   • scissors

가위 •   • cutting board

전자레인지 •   • knife

밥솥 •   • gas range

칼 •   • frying pan

도마 •   • pot

국자 •   • rice cooker

Look at the kitchen tools and write their names in the spaces provided.

프	스	팬	이	가	라

전	국	솥	자	밥	칼

비	주	방	도	구	냄

가	스	마	국	자	도

형, 얼굴 각도 이렇게 나와야 돼요.

[hyeong eol-gul gak-do i-reo-ke na-wa-ya dwae-yo]

The angle of your face

needs to come out like this.

Let's learn the names of body parts. Trace the words and practice writing them in the blank spaces.

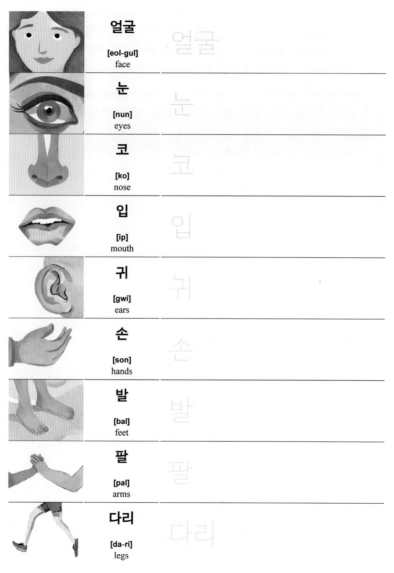

	얼굴 [eol-gul] face	얼굴
	눈 [nun] eyes	눈
	코 [ko] nose	코
	입 [ip] mouth	입
	귀 [gwi] ears	귀
	손 [son] hands	손
	발 [bal] feet	발
	팔 [pal] arms	팔
	다리 [da-ri] legs	다리

Practice words

> **런쥔이의 코가 진짜 예뻐.**
> RENJUN's nose is really cute.

> **얼굴 중에서 눈이 제일 예뻐.**
> The eyes are the prettiest part of my face.

> **귀가 시려워요.**
> My ears feel cold.

> **손이 시려워 꽁, 발이 시려워 꽁.**
> My hands are cold, my feet are cold.

'시리다' is a Korean word that is often used to describe a physical sensation of coldness or chill, especially in reference to parts of the body, like fingers or toes, when they feel cold to the point of being painful or uncomfortable.

▸ **각 단어와 한글을 연결해 보세요.** Match each word to the correct Korean.

얼굴 •	• legs
눈 •	• feet
코 •	• hands
입 •	• nose
귀 •	• eyes
손 •	• arms
발 •	• mouth
팔 •	• face
다리 •	• ears

Choose the appropriate word from the options to fill in the blank.

보기 눈, 코, 입, 손, 발, 팔, 다리

YUTA | 우리가 아직까지 좀 할 게 남았거든요

눈썹도 좀 올려 줘야 돼.

[nun-sseop-do jom ol-lyeo jwo-ya dwae]

You need to raise your eyebrows too.

▸ 새로운 단어 배우기 New Words

Let's learn the names of body parts. Trace the words and freely practice in the blank spaces.

	손바닥 [son-ppa-dak] palm	손바닥
	손가락 [son-kka-rak] fingers	손가락
	발바닥 [bal-ppa-dak] sole	발바닥
	발가락 [bal-kka-rak] toes	발가락
	손톱 [son-top] fingernails	손톱
	보조개 [bo-jo-gae] dimple	보조개
	쌍꺼풀 [ssang-kkeo-pul] double eyelids	쌍꺼풀
	눈썹 [nun-sseop] eyebrows	눈썹
	속눈썹 [song-nun-sseop] eyelashes	속눈썹

 Practice words

손톱이 가늘고 길어요.
My fingernails are thin and long.

발가락이 가늘고 길어요.
My toes are thin and long.

손가락이 굵어 반지가 안 들어가요.
My fingers are too thick for the ring to fit.

보조개가 있는 사람이 좋아요.
I like people who have dimples.

'길다[gilda]' is a Korean word that indicates a long state of length. This word is used when the physical length of something is longer than average. For example, '손톱이 길다[sontobi gilda]' means that the fingernails are longer than what is typically seen, and '발가락이 길다[balgaragi gilda]' is used to describe toes that are longer than other people.

▸ **각 단어와 한글을 연결해 보세요.** Match each word to the correct Korean.

손바닥 •	• eyelashes
손가락 •	• eyebrows
발바닥 •	• double eyelids
손톱 •	• dimple
발가락 •	• palm
보조개 •	• fingers
쌍꺼풀 •	• sole
눈썹 •	• toes
속눈썹 •	• fingernails

Look at the pictures and write the opposite word.

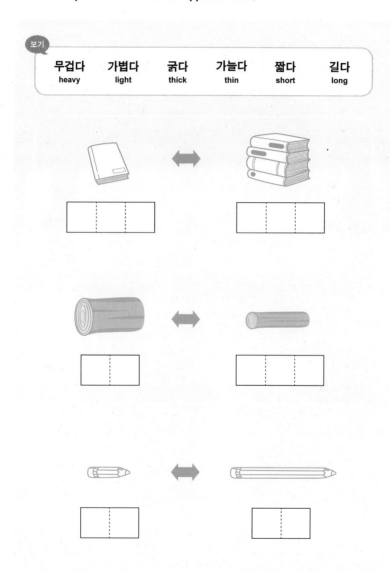

보기

| 무겁다 | 가볍다 | 굵다 | 가늘다 | 짧다 | 길다 |
| heavy | light | thick | thin | short | long |

CHAPTER 5

NCT's CULTURE

그렇네요 NCT 127에 발렌타인 보이가 있다고 들어가지고

그리고 김도영 씨?

[geu-ri-go Gim-Do-Yeong ssi?]

Also, KIM DOYOUNG?

182

▶ 새로운 단어 배우기 New Words

Let's learn Korean honorifics and pronouns. Trace the words and freely practice in the blank spaces.

	-씨 [-ssi] Mr / Mrs	-씨
	-님 [-nim] Mr / Mrs(respectable)	-님
Hey!	**야** [ya] hey	야
	나 [na] I	나
	너/당신 [neo/dang-sin] you	너/당신
	그 [geu] he	그
	그녀 [geu-nyeo] she	그녀
	아주머니 [a-ju-meo-ni] ma'am	아주머니
	아저씨 [a-jeo-ssi] sir	아저씨

Practice words

도영 씨, 안녕하세요.
Hello, DOYOUNG.

해찬 님, 들어오세요.
Please come in, HAECHAN.

야, 뭐 해?
Hey, what are you doing?

아저씨, 잘 지내셨어요?
Sir, how have you been?

'-야' is used to call someone's name casually. Add '-야' to names without final consonants like '민수야', and '-아' to names with final consonants like '지은아'.

▸ **각 단어와 한글을 연결해 보세요.** Match each word to the correct Korean.

-씨 •   • sir

나 •   • ma'am

너 •   • -nim

아주머니 •   • she

아저씨 •   • he

-님 •   • you

그 •   • hey

그녀 •   • Mr, Mrs

야 •   • I

선생님

Seonsaengnim

Foreigners are often surprised by the frequent use of the term "teacher" in Korea because the Korean system of honorifics reflects a very specific and hierarchical culture. "Teacher" is used not only for educators but also for doctors, lawyers, or experts in any field as a way to express respect for their social status or esteem.

For example, while all educators are referred to as "teacher" in the education sector, in Western cultures, honorifics are usually limited to titles like Mr., Mrs., or Ms. followed by a surname or first name, like Mr., Mrs., or Ms. Additionally, in Korea, it's common to use "teacher" more universally for older individuals or those with higher social status, which can seem unusual and surprising to foreigners.

Therefore, when explaining the Korean system of honorifics, it's important to highlight these cultural differences and the meanings and expressions of respect that these titles convey. This helps greatly in understanding the mutual respect and etiquette in Korea.

쟈니 형이다.

[Jya-ni hyeong-i-da]

It's JOHNNY.

Let's learn about family titles. Trace the words and freely practice in the blank spaces.

할머니
[hal-meo-ni]
grandmother

할아버지
[hal-a-beo-ji]
grandfather

엄마
[eom-ma]
mother

아빠
[a-ppa]
father

형
[hyeong]
older brother(used by males)

오빠
[o-ppa]
older brother(used by females)

누나
[nu-na]
older sister(used by males)

언니
[eon-ni]
older sister(used by females)

동생
[dong-saeng]
younger sibling

Practice words

엄마가 부엌에서 요리하세요.
My mom is cooking in the kitchen.

할아버지는 방에서 주무세요.
My grandfather is sleeping in the room.

나는 누나가 한 명 있어.
I have one older sister.

동생은 고등학생이에요.
My younger sibling is a high school student.

Let's look at honorific words: The honorific for '자다'(sleep) is '주무시다', for '먹다.마시다'(eat/drink) is '드시다', and for '있다'(exist) is '계시다'.

If the subject is your younger sibling, you say "동생은 방에서 자요"(My brother sleeps in his room) but if it's grandfather, you should say respectfully "할아버지는 방에서 주무세요"(Grandfather is sleeping in the room).

▸ **각 단어와 한글을 연결해 보세요.** Match each word to the correct Korean.

엄마 •	• younger sibling
아빠 •	• older sister
할머니 •	• older brother
할아버지 •	• grandmother
누나 •	• grandfather
형 •	• mother
동생 •	• father
언니 •	• older brother (female)
오빠 •	• older sister (female)

▶가족 관계도 Family terms

Learn the family titles in Korean.

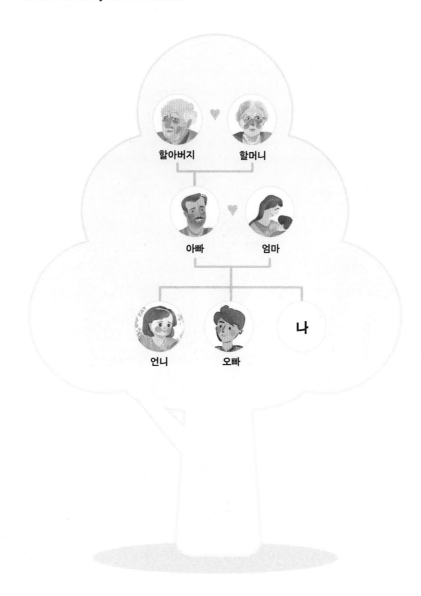

Check through video

그러면 형은 무슨 영화 좋아해요?

[geu-reo-myeon hyeong-eun mu-seun yeong-hwa jo-a-hae-yo?]

What kind of movies do you like?

NCT Korean Vocabulary note

Let's learn entertainment and performance-related terms. Trace the words and freely practice in the blank spaces.

영화
[yeong-hwa]
movie

영화

영화배우
[yeong-hwa-bae-u]
actor/actress

영화배우

예매하다
[ye-mae-ha-da]
book/reserve

예매하다

좌석
[jwa-seok]
seat

좌석

연극
[yeon-geuk]
play

연극

표
[pyo]
ticket

표

뮤지컬
[myu-ji-keol]
musical

뮤지컬

입장권
[ip-jjang-kkwon]
admission ticket

입장권

초대장
[cho-dae-jjang]
invitation

초대장

Practice
words

우리 **영화** 많이
사랑해 주세요.
Please love and support our movie.

입장권과 신분증
준비하세요.
Please have your ticket and ID ready.

도영이 형이 **뮤지컬** 데뷔했어.
DOYOUNG made his musical debut.

초대장 받았어요.
I received an invitation.

Foreign language+하다[hada]' indicates the action or activity of using a foreign language in Korean. It is mainly used when expressing or combining Korean with English words or sentences. This expression emphasizes the active utilization of a foreign language, often seen in trendy or specific fields. For example, phrases like "가수로 데뷔하다"(Debut as a singer) or "팬들과 채팅하다"(Chat with fans) demonstrate this usage.

▸ **각 단어와 한글을 연결해 보세요.** Match each word to the correct Korean.

영화 ·   · musical

영화배우 ·   · ticket

입장권 ·   · movie

초대장 ·   · seat

좌석 ·   · book

연극 ·   · admission ticket

표 ·   · actor/actress

예매하다 ·   · invitation

뮤지컬 ·   · play

Match the words to the verbs and write down the sentences below.

영화(를)
movie

받다
receive

표(를)
ticket

좋아하다
like

초대장(을)
invitation

앉다
take

좌석(에)
seat

준비하다
prepare

를

를

을

에

폴라로이드로 찍자.

[pol-ra-ro-i-deu-ro jjik-ja]

Let's take a polaroid picture.

Let's learn words related to media. Trace the words and freely practice in the blank spaces.

NEW DRAMA 드라마	**드라마** [deu-la-ma] drama	드라마
	연기하다 [yeon-gi-ha-da] to act	연기하다
	연기자 [yeon-gi-ja] actor	연기자
	대본 [dae-bon] script	대본
	남자 주인공 [nam-ja ju-in-gong] male lead	남자 주인공
	여자 주인공 [yeo-ja ju-in-gong] female lead	여자 주인공
	등장인물 [deung-jang-in-mul] character	등장인물
	찍다 [jjik-da] to film	찍다
	무대 [mu-dae] stage	무대

Practice words

오늘 **드라마** 오디션을 봤어요.
I had a drama audition today.

대본 연습하고 있어요.
I'm practicing the script.

시즈니들의 **무대**예요.
It's the stage of NCTzen.

NCT 이번 **무대 찢었다.**
NCT killed this performance.

'**찢었다**[Jjijeotda]'(tore it up) is one of the new slang words used when someone does something extremely well or leaves a strong impression. While '**찢다** [jjitda]'(tear) originally means physically tearing something, when used in contexts like stage performances, shows, or games, it means 'did overwhelmingly well.'

▸ **각 단어와 한글을 연결해 보세요.** Match each word to the correct Korean.

드라마 •	• stage
남자 주인공 •	• character
여자 주인공 •	• actor
연기하다 •	• script
대본 •	• to film
연기자 •	• female lead
찢다 •	• male lead
등장인물 •	• to act
무대 •	• drama

Please fill in the blank spaces so that Korean characters do not overlap in horizontal and vertical lines.

〈주인공〉

〈연기자〉

〈초대장〉

〈입장권〉

Check through video

안녕하십니까, 앵커 제노입니다.

[an-nyeong-ha-sim-ni-kka, aeng-keo Je-no-im-ni-da]

Hello, this is anchor JENO.

NCT Korean Vocabulary note

Let's learn words related to media. Trace the words and freely practice in the blank spaces.

	앵커 [aeng-keo] anchor	앵커
	신문 [sin-mun] newspaper	신문
	라디오 [ra-di-o] radio	라디오
	광고 [gwang-go] advertisement	광고
	뉴스 [nyu-seu] news	뉴스
	방송 [bang-song] broadcasting	방송
	방송국 [bang-song-guk] broadcasting station	방송국
	신문사 [sin-mun-sa] newspaper company	신문사
	잡지 [jap-jji] magazine	잡지

Practice words

신문에 우리가 나왔어.
We appeared in the newspaper.

오늘 음방(음악 방송) 컴백해요.
We're making our comeback on music show today.

저희 교복 입고 광고 찍었어요.
We filmed a commercial wearing our school uniforms.

잡지 화보를 촬영했어요.
We did a magazine photoshoot.

'찍다[jjikda]'(shoot) generally refers to the act of taking photographs or videos. Typically, it involves using a handheld camera or smartphone to capture images or record footage. '촬영하다[choryeonghada]'(film) on the other hand, is a more specialized term often used in the context of producing video works such as movies or dramas.

▸ **각 단어와 한글을 연결해 보세요.** Match each word to the correct Korean.

앵커 •　　　　　　　　• magazine

방송국 •　　　　　　　• radio

라디오 •　　　　　　　• anchor

신문 •　　　　　　　　• advertisement

뉴스 •　　　　　　　　• broadcasting

광고 •　　　　　　　　• broadcasting station

잡지 •　　　　　　　　• newspaper

방송 •　　　　　　　　• news

신문사 •　　　　　　　• newspaper company

Let's explore the journey that NCT has taken so far.

1 〉 2016년 4월 9일 〉

NCT U 데뷔. 첫 유닛 NCT U가 싱글 "The 7th Sense"와 "Without You"로 데뷔.

2 〉 2016년 7월 7일 〉

NCT 127 데뷔. NCT 127이 첫 미니앨범 "NCT #127"로 데뷔.

3 〉 2016년 8월 24일 〉

NCT DREAM 데뷔. 청소년 유닛 NCT DREAM이 싱글 "Chewing Gum"으로 데뷔.

4 〉 2019년 1월 17일 〉

WayV 데뷔. 중국을 기반으로 한 유닛 WayV가 싱글 "The Vision"으로 데뷔.

Check through video

고등학교 때지?

[go-deung-hak-kkyo ttae-ji?]

That was in high school, right?

NCT Korean Vocabulary note

Let's learn about educational institutions. Trace the words and freely practice in the blank spaces.

어린이집
[eo-ri-ni-jip]
daycare center

유치원
[yu-chi-won]
kindergarten

초등학교
[cho-deung-hak-kkyo]
elementary school

중학교
[jung-hak-kkyo]
middle school

고등학교
[go-deung-hak-kkyo]
high school

대학교
[dae-hak-kkyo]
university

대학원
[dae-ha-gwon]
graduate school

학원
[ha-gwon]
cram school

도서관
[do-seo-gwan]
library

Practice words

재현이 형은 유치원 때도 잘생겼어.
JAEHYUN was good-looking even when he was in kindergarten.

나는 중학교 때 SM 연습생이 되었어.
I became a SM trainee when I was in middle school.

저는 캐나다에서 초등학교를 다녔어요.
I went to elementary school in Canada.

시즈니들, 시티고등학교로 놀러오세요.
NCTzens, come visit CITY High School.

"학교를 다니다"(Going to school) means being enrolled in a school and receiving education, essentially going to school regularly to pursue academic activities. The phrase "학교에 가다"(Go to school) can also be used in the same context.

▸ **각 단어와 한글을 연결해 보세요.** Match each word to the correct Korean.

유치원 ·   · elementary school

어린이집 ·   · university

초등학교 ·   · cram school

중학교 ·   · kindergarten

고등학교 ·   · graduate school

대학교 ·   · middle school

대학원 ·   · high school

학원 ·   · daycare center

도서관 ·   · library

Find the words below hidden in the puzzle.

보기

| 유치원 | 초등학교 | 고등학교 | 대학원 |
| 어린이집 | 중학교 | 대학교 | 학원 |

상	상	하	다	연	습	생	시	절	쿤
굿	어	린	이	집	잘	생	기	다	대
모	가	족	이	되	어	주	인	공	학
닝	초	등	학	교	마	크	유	치	원
도	서	실	장	문	무	대	오	르	다
서	울	초	대	학	교	의	댄	스	짱
관	우	등	생	은	연	습	스	스	로
텐	중	학	교	엔	고	등	학	교	실
도	서	관	에	가	는	날	원	장	님
시	티	하	이	스	쿨	일	이	칠	반

HENDERY 춤 잘 추고 왜냐면

키 크고 춤 잘 추고 되게 좋아요.

[ki keu-go chum jal chu-go doe-ge jo-a-yo]

JISUNG is tall, dances well, and...he's just great!

▸ 새로운 단어 배우기 New Words

Let's learn words related to idol culture. Trace the words and freely practice in the blank spaces.

아이돌
[a-i-dol]
idol

아이돌

팬클럽
[paen-keul-leob]
fan club

팬클럽

응원봉
[eung-won-bong]
light stick

응원봉

뮤직비디오
[myu-jik-bi-di-o]
music video

뮤직비디오

앨범
[ael-beom]
album

앨범

노래
[no-rae]
song

노래

춤
[chum]
dance

춤

콘서트
[kon-seo-teu]
concert

콘서트

가사
[ga-sa]
lyrics

가사

Practice words

▶ **주요 표현을 배워 보세요.** Learn key expressions.

NCT 팬클럽 이름은
NCTzen!
The name of NCT's fan club is NCTzen!

응원봉 아니고 몸뭔봄!
It's not a light stick,
it's a Meommeonbom!

이번 앨범도 최선을
다했어요.
We did our best for this
album too.

신곡 노래 가사가
정말 좋아요.
The lyrics of the new song are
really good.

"최선을 다하다"(Doing one's best) means putting forth maximum effort when doing something. It involves striving for the best possible outcome in a given task. This expression emphasizes effort and dedication, reflecting a determination to persevere and not give up, regardless of the circumstances.

▶ **각 단어와 한글을 연결해 보세요.** Match each word to the correct Korean.

아이돌 •   • concert

응원봉 •   • music video

팬클럽 •   • lyrics

춤 •   • song

노래 •   • light stick

가사 •   • album

앨범 •   • idol

콘서트 •   • fan club

뮤직비디오 •   • dance

Create a light stick name using Korean consonants. Following the example, combine your favorite member's initials with 'Bongbong' using the consonants provided below.

카메라를 버릴 때가 있어요.

[ka-me-ra-reul beo-ril ttae-ga it-sseo-yo]

I sometimes put my camera away at times.

▸ 새로운 단어 배우기 New Words

Let's learn words related to recycling. Trace the words and freely practice in the blank spaces.

유리병
[yu-ri-beong]
glass bottle

유리병

플라스틱
[peul-la-seu-tik]
plastic

플라스틱

캔
[kaen]
can

캔

비닐
[bi-nil]
plastic bag

비닐

음식물 쓰레기
[eum-sing-mul sseu-re-gi]
food waste

음식물 쓰레기

종이
[jong-i]
paper

종이

쓰레기
[sseu-re-gi]
trash

쓰레기

버리다
[beo-ri-da]
to dispose of

버리다

재활용
[jae-hwa-ryong]
recycling

재활용

Practice words

플라스틱은 어디에 버려?
Where do I throw away plastic?

이것은 '일반 쓰레기'입니까?
Is this 'trash'?

재활용 분리하기 어렵다.
Separating recyclables is difficult.

비닐은 따로 모아 주세요.
Please collect the plastic bag separately.

'따로[ttaro]' in Korean indicates that two or more things or situations are separated or distinct from each other. Generally, it implies that two or more things are handled or treated separately. It can sometimes denote that optional items are dealt with independently.

▶ **각 단어와 한글을 연결해 보세요.** Match each word to the correct Korean.

종이 ·   · plastic

비닐 ·   · trash

유리병 ·   · to dispose of

캔 ·   · paper

재활용 ·   · plastic bag

음식물 쓰레기 ·   · glass bottle

쓰레기 ·   · can

버리다 ·   · food waste

플라스틱 ·   · recycling

Look at the picture and the initial consonants, then guess the word.

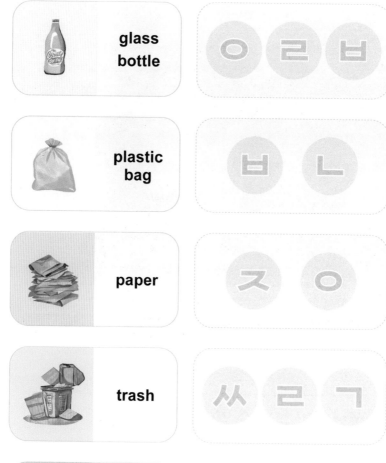

	glass bottle	ㅇ ㄹ ㅂ
	plastic bag	ㅂ ㄴ
	paper	ㅈ ㅇ
	trash	ㅆ ㄹ ㄱ

 recycling

ㅈ ㅎ ㅇ

NCT's
KOREAN
VOCABULARY
NOTE

Check through video

✳ 도영 ISFJ　　　　설날 문자 보낼 수 있어?

설날 문자 보낼 수 있어?

[seol-lal mun-ja bo-nael su it-sseo?]

Can you text Happy Seollal texts?

Let's learn about Korean cultural traditions. Trace the words and freely practice in the blank spaces.

궁
[gung]
palace

궁

한복
[han-bok]
hanbok

한복

갓
[gat]
gat

갓

설날
[seol-lal]
Korean New Year

설날

윷놀이
[yun-no-ri]
yutnori

윷놀이

한옥
[ha-nok]
hanok

한옥

부채춤
[bu-chae-chum]
fan dance

부채춤

떡국
[tteok-kkuk]
rice cake soup

떡국

제기차기
[je-gi-cha-gi]
jegichagi

제기차기

 Practice words

궁에서 찍은 뮤직비디오 봤어?
Have you seen the music video filmed at the palace?

윷놀이 해 봤어?
Have you played yutnori before?

오늘 설날인데 할아버지께 연락드리자.
Let's call grandfather to wish him a Happy New Year.

한복이 잘 어울려요.
The hanbok suits on you.

'설날[Seollal]' is one of the most representative traditional holidays in Korea, falling on the 1st day of the 1st lunar month. On this day, it is customary to send greetings to family and relatives. This is called '설날 안부 문자[Seollal Anbu Munja]', and the messages usually include wishes like "새해 복 많이 받으세요 [Saehae bok mani badeuseyo]"(Happy New Year).

▸ **각 단어와 한글을 연결해 보세요.** Match each word to the correct Korean.

한복 •	• fan dance
한옥 •	• palace
윷놀이 •	• jegichagi
궁 •	• hanbok
부채춤 •	• hanok
제기차기 •	• gat
떡국 •	• Korean New Year
설날 •	• rice cake soup
갓 •	• yutnori

설명

Yutnori is a traditional Korean board game played with wooden sticks by two or more players.

도 [do]
one forward

개 [gae]
two forward

걸 [geol]
three forward

윷 [yut]
four forward/
one more

모 [mo]
five forward/
one more

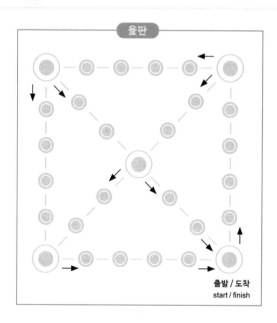

윷판

출발 / 도착
start / finish

⑩ 기념일 gi-nyeom-il

이렇게 생일 축하해 주는 게 어디 있어.

[i-reo-ke saeng-il chu-ka-hae ju-neun ge eo-di it-sseo]

Nobody celebrates a birthday like this.

Let's learn Korean holidays and special occasions. Trace the words and freely practice in the blank spaces.

	백일 [bae-gil] 100th day celebration	백일
	생일 [saeng-il] birthday	생일
	한글날 [han-geul-lal] Hangeul Day	한글날
	광복절 [gwang-bok-jjeol] National Liberation Day	광복절
	개천절 [gae-cheon-jeol] National Foundation Day	개천절
	어버이날 [eo-beo-i-nal] Parents' Day	어버이날
	어린이날 [eo-ri-ni-nal] Children's Day	어린이날
	삼일절 [sam-il-jjeol] Independence Movement Day	삼일절
	현충일 [hyeon-chung-il] Memorial Day	현충일

Practice words

조카 **백일** 선물로 뭐가 좋을까?
What would be good as a 100th day gift for my nephew?

광복절에 태극기를 달았어요.
I hung the Taegukgi on National Liberation Day.

오늘은 **한글날**이에요.
Today is Hangeul Day.

어린이날인데 선물 주세요.
It's Children's Day, so please give me a present.

'**백일[Baegil]**'(100th day celebration) is a traditional Korean celebration of a baby's 100th day. In the past, when infant survival rates were low, reaching 100 days healthy had great significance, so families celebrated baegil to pray for the baby's health. Even now, families gather for the 100th-day celebration, take special photos of the baby, and prepare special foods.

▸ **각 단어와 한글을 연결해 보세요.** Match each word to the correct Korean.

백일 •
생일 •
개천절 •
광복절 •
한글날 •
어버이날 •
어린이날 •
삼일절 •
현충일 •

• Parents' Day
• Children's Day
• Independence Movement Day
• Memorial Day
• birthday
• Hangeul Day
• National Liberation Day
• National Foundation Day
• 100th day celebration

220

Please answer the questions below.

1. **NCT 127의 데뷔일은 언제인가요?**
   What was NCT 127's debut date?

   ① 6월 6일
   ② 7월 7일
   ③ 8월 8일
   ④ 9월 9일
   ⑤ 10월 10일

이름 Name:

점수 Score:

2. **NCT DREAM의 데뷔일은 언제인가요?**
   What was NCT DREAM's debut date?

   ① 1월 25일
   ② 3월 15일
   ③ 5월 5일
   ④ 8월 15일
   ⑤ 8월 25일

3. **NCT 127이 데뷔 8주년 팬미팅을 한 장소는?**
   Where was NCT 127's 8th anniversary fan meeting held?

   ① 고척스카이돔 Gocheok Sky Dome
   ② 인천아시아드주경기장 Incheon Asiad Main Stadium
   ③ 잠실실내체육관 Jamsil Indoor Stadium
   ④ 올림픽체조경기장 Olympic Gymnastics Arena
   ⑤ 월드컵경기장 World Cup Stadium

4. **WayV의 데뷔일은 언제인가요?**
   What was WayV debut date?

   ① 1월 17일
   ② 2월 7일
   ③ 8월 25일
   ④ 9월 1일
   ⑤ 4월 5일

ANSWERS

Answers 답안

p.16

김밥 • • tteokbokki
된장찌개 • • gimbap
떡볶이 • • grilled pork belly
불고기 • • bulgogi
삼겹살 • • kimchi stew
비빔밥 • • kimchi
김치찌개 • • bibimbap
김치 • • rice
밥 • • soybean paste stew

p.17

일 SUN	월 MON	화 TUE	수 WED	목 THU	금 FRI	토 SAT
1주						

김치찌개
2주

3주

4주

5주

p.20

귤 • • strawberry
수박 • • apple
바나나 • • grape
사과 • • mandarin
배 • • mango
딸기 • • banana
포도 • • watermelon
망고 • • peach
복숭아 • • pear

p.21

과	일	나	라	가	바	나	나
귤	라	딸	면	방	고	재	마
마	바	기	먹	노	래	민	사
포	도	우	자	두	망	고	랑
체	리	유	파	인	애	플	해
도	수	박	소	금	사	빵	요
레	파	솔	라	시	과	태	배
미	감	복	숭	아	마	크	텐

p.24

아이스크림 • • chocolate
떡 • • coffee
빵 • • candy
사탕 • • ice cream
초콜릿 • • snack
과자 • • bread
케이크 • • biscuit
커피 • • rice cake
간식 • • cake

p.25

제노

쟈니

과자snacks
아이스크림ice cream

태용

유타

도영

텐

Answers 답안

p.28

즐겁다	happy
웃다	funny
행복하다	pleasant
편안하다	sorry
재미있다	tremble
슬프다	scary
무섭다	laugh
떨리다	comfortable
미안하다	sad

p.29

오늘 하루 잘 보내셨나요?
How was your day?

오늘 최고, 좋은 하루! (좋다)
Today was the best, what a great day!

콘서트에서 여러분을 만나 행복해요. (행복하다)
I'm happy to meet you all at the concert.

시즈니와 함께해서 정말 행복하고 좋아요.
I really like and am happy with NCTzens too.

안녕하세요.

오늘 최고의 하루였어요.

NCT 콘서트에 다녀와

너무 기쁘고 행복해요.

---

p.32

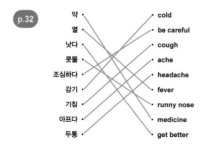

약	cold
열	be careful
낫다	cough
콧물	ache
조심하다	headache
감기	fever
기침	runny nose
아프다	medicine
두통	get better

p.33

p.36

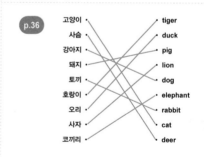

고양이	tiger
사슴	duck
강아지	pig
돼지	lion
토끼	dog
호랑이	elephant
오리	rabbit
사자	cat
코끼리	deer

p.37

도영 **토 끼**

재현 **고 양 이**

정우 **강 아 지**

마크 **치 타**

양양 **양**

해찬 **곰**

p.40

흐리다 •	• chilly
습하다 •	• hot
따뜻하다 •	• cloudy
쌀쌀하다 •	• warm
맑다 •	• cold
춥다 •	• humid
덥다 •	• clear
좋다 •	• fine / good
나쁘다 •	• bad

p.41

오늘 날씨가 좋다 .

날씨가 나쁘다 .

하늘이 흐려서 비가 올 것 같아요.

해가 비쳐서 따뜻하다 .

날씨가 더워서 아이스크림이 먹고 싶어.

바람이 불어 쌀쌀하다 .

눈도 오고 너무 춥다 .

p.44

어제 •	• tomorrow
올해 •	• next week
작년 •	• today
내일 •	• this year
이번 주 •	• yesterday
오늘 •	• next year
지난주 •	• this week
내년 •	• last year
다음 주 •	• last week

p.48

점심 •	• evening
새벽 •	• weekend
아침 •	• holiday
주말 •	• dawn
공휴일 •	• night
저녁 •	• morning
밤 •	• lunch
낮 •	• weekday
평일 •	• day

p.49

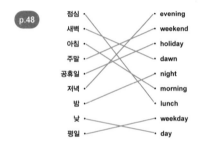

가	나	다	라	마	바	사	월	요	일
엔	시	티	콘	서	트	아	침	창	가
수	산	들	바	람	저	녁	약	그	림
요	금	밤	양	갱	보	이	속	편	가
일	나	는	새	벽	비	주	시	지	족
고	눈	부	신	하	늘	말	간	구	름
구	평	사	원	무	지	개	점	심	밥
마	일	봄	소	풍	공	휴	일	식	사
화	요	일	모	래	시	계	가	을	날
앨	범	누	리	집	한	국	어	공	부

Answers 답안

p.52

듣다 • • go
말하다 • • listen / hear
가다 • • come
보다 • • sleep
읽다 • • walk
먹다 • • see
자다 • • say / tell
걷다 • • read
오다 • • eat

p.62

소고기 • • sugar
계란 • • soy sauce
돼지고기 • • beef
두부 • • soybean paste
된장 • • pork
고추장 • • eggs
간장 • • salt
설탕 • • tofu
소금 • • hot pepper paste

p.53

유튜브 보기 / 잠자기 / 카페 가기 / 일어나기 / 음악 듣기 / 밥 먹기 / 산책 / 운동하기 / 책 읽기

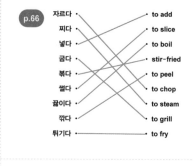

p.66

자르다 • • to add
찌다 • • to slice
넣다 • • to boil
굽다 • • stir-fried
볶다 • • to peel
썰다 • • to chop
끓이다 • • to steam
깎다 • • to grill
튀기다 • • to fry

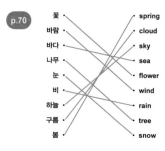

p.70

꽃 • • spring
바람 • • cloud
바다 • • sky
나무 • • sea
눈 • • flower
비 • • wind
하늘 • • rain
구름 • • tree
봄 • • snow

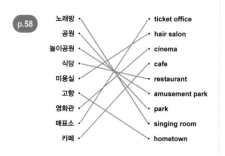

p.58

노래방 • • ticket office
공원 • • hair salon
놀이공원 • • cinema
식당 • • cafe
미용실 • • restaurant
고향 • • amusement park
영화관 • • park
매표소 • • singing room
카페 • • hometown

Answers 답안

p.71

- 우리나라는 더워요.
- 바다가 있어 수영할 수 있어요.
- 파란 하늘이 최고예요.

p.78

기차 • — • terminal
배 • — • airport
비행기 • — • car
버스 • — • train
택시 • — • boat
공항 • — • bicycle
자전거 • — • bus
자동차 • — • airplane
터미널 • — • taxi

p.74

지하철역 • — • apartment
도로 / 길 • — • crosswalk
아파트 • — • subway station
횡단보도 • — • road
정류장 • — • traffic light
나리 • — • building
신호등 • — • bus stop
빌딩 • — • bridge
편의점 • — • convenience store

p.79

보기

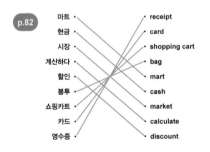

배   기차   버스   택시   자전거

p.82

마트 • — • receipt
현금 • — • card
시장 • — • shopping cart
계산하다 • — • bag
할인 • — • mart
봉투 • — • cash
쇼핑카트 • — • market
카드 • — • calculate
영수증 • — • discount

p.75

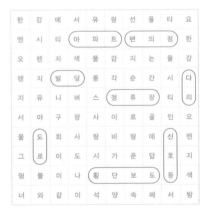

한	강	에	서	유	람	선	을	타	요
엔	시	티	아	파	트	편	의	점	한
오	렌	지	색	물	감	지	는	울	강
렌	지	빌	딩	통	각	순	간	시	다
지	유	니	버	스	정	류	장	티	리
서	야	구	장	사	이	로	골	인	오
올	도	회	사	람	바	람	에	신	렌
그	로	이	도	시	가	준	답	호	지
럼	불	이	나	횡	단	보	도	등	색
너	와	같	이	석	양	속	에	서	밤

p.86

취소하다 • — • breakfast
풀다 • — • stay
싸다 • — • cancel
예약하다 • — • pack
묵다 • — • unpack
조식 • — • make a reservation
맡기다 • — • luggage
빈방 • — • leave
짐 • — • vacancy

p.87

1. ④   2. ②   3. ⑤

4. ⑤   5. 5명

p.90

취미	music
등산	reading
게임	photography
영화 감상	hobby
독서	watching movies
운동	drawing
사진	game
음악	hiking
그림	exercise

p.91

NCT Hobby Report

NAME 재민	NAME 정우
HOBBY 사진	HOBBY
NAME 해찬	NAME 태용
HOBBY	HOBBY
NAME 윈윈	NAME 텐
HOBBY	HOBBY
NAME 도영	NAME 유타
HOBBY	HOBBY
NAME 재현	NAME 쟈니
HOBBY	HOBBY

p.94

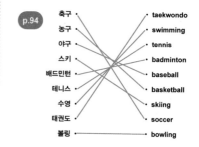

축구	taekwondo
농구	swimming
야구	tennis
스키	badminton
배드민턴	baseball
테니스	basketball
수영	skiing
태권도	soccer
볼링	bowling

p.95

NCT Exercise Report

NAME 재민	NAME 양양
EXERCISE 배드민턴	EXERCISE
NAME 샤오쥔	NAME 마크
EXERCISE	EXERCISE
NAME 천러	NAME 제노
EXERCISE	EXERCISE
NAME 지성	NAME 핸드리
EXERCISE	EXERCISE
NAME 정우	NAME 해찬
EXERCISE	EXERCISE

p.100

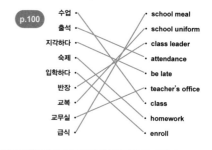

수업	school meal
출석	school uniform
지각하다	class leader
숙제	attendance
입학하다	be late
반장	teacher's office
교복	class
교무실	homework
급식	enroll

Answers 답안

p.101

교장 principal	교감 communion	담임 homeroom teacher
마크	sticker	sticker

반장 class leader	체육부장 athletic director	청소부장 class cleaning director
sticker	sticker	sticker

봉사부장 service coordinator	총무 administrative director	도서부장 library director
sticker	sticker	sticker

p.104

학생 · · doctor
선생님 · · chef
회사원 · · nurse
의사 · · police officer
간호사 · · teacher
경찰 · · athlete
소방관 · · student
운동선수 · · firefighter
요리사 · · office worker

p.108

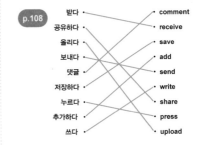

받다 · · comment
공유하다 · · receive
올리다 · · save
보내다 · · add
댓글 · · send
저장하다 · · write
누르다 · · share
추가하다 · · press
쓰다 · · upload

p.109

사진 올리기

p.112

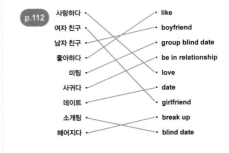

사랑하다 · · like
여자 친구 · · boyfriend
남자 친구 · · group blind date
좋아하다 · · be in relationship
미팅 · · love
사귀다 · · date
데이트 · · girlfriend
소개팅 · · break up
헤어지다 · · blind date

p.116

놀다 · · friendship
만나다 · · fight
우정 · · cherish
싸우다 · · be close
부르다 · · play
친하다 · · meet
소중하다 · · call
화해하다 · · bring along
데려오다 · · reconcile

p.117

지	금	우	리	함	께	노	래	해	요
놀	면	추	우	리	의	말	만	나	다
다	정	억	정	성	스	러	운	음	즐
지	금	의	나	에	게	소	나	기	거
공	기	만	두	려	운	중	서	로	운
너	와	남	이	떨	림	하	조	명	화
싸	우	다	가	부	르	다	웃	음	해
내	일	어	제	친	구	와	소	풍	하
모	두	친	하	다	이	간	편	하	다
좋	다	구	서	로	가	좋	은	이	웃

p.120

맛없다 — delicious
시다 — bitter
달다 — salty
맛있다 — sweet
쓰다 — sour
고소하다 — tasteless
맵다 — spicy
싱겁다 — nutty
짜다 — not salty enough

p.121

sweet — 달 다

spicy — 맵 다

salty — 짜 다

sour — 시 다

bitter — 쓰 다

p.124

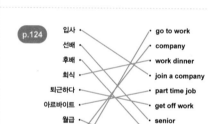

입사 — go to work
선배 — company
후배 — work dinner
회식 — join a company
퇴근하다 — part time job
아르바이트 — get off work
월급 — senior
회사 — junior
출근 — monthly salary

p.128

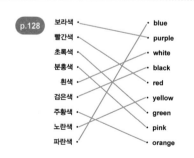

보라색 — blue
빨간색 — purple
초록색 — white
분홍색 — black
흰색 — red
검은색 — yellow
주황색 — green
노란색 — pink
파란색 — orange

Answers 답안

p.129

 런쥔 제노 재민

색 __노란색__

 천러 쟈니 웬드리

색 ....

 해찬 쿤 양양

색 ....

p.132

뚱뚱하다 — overweight
잘생기다 — handsome
예쁘다 — pretty
귀엽다 — cute
작다 — small
날씬하다 — slim
못생기다 — ugly
크다 — big
아름답다 — beautiful

big / cute / ugly / small / beautiful / overweight / handsome / slim / pretty

p.136

쇼핑하다 — to shop
싸다 — cheap
사다 — to buy
가격 — price
비싸다 — expensive
교환하다 — to exchange
사이즈 — size
깎다 — discount
포장하다 — to wrap

to wrap / expensive / cheap / discount / size / to buy / price / to exchange / to shop

p.142

거울 — mirror
소파 — sofa
옷장 — wardrobe
식탁 — dining table
텔레비전 — television
선풍기 — fan
책장 — bookshelf
에어컨 — air conditioner
침대 — bed

p.143

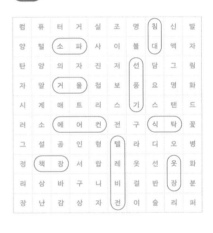

p.146

복사기 — photocopier
명함 — business card
서류 — document
회의실 — conference room
서랍 — drawer
도장 — stamp
슬리퍼 — slippers
전화기 — telephone
컴퓨터 — computer

Answers 답안

p.147

편지 letter		사용하다 to use
명함 business card		받다 receive
펜 pen		쓰다 to write
컴퓨터 computer		내려받다 download

편지를 쓰다

명함을 받다

펜을 사용하다

컴퓨터로 내려받다

p.150

샴푸		shower
린스		soap
세면대		bathtub
수건		shampoo
칫솔		hair conditioner
치약		towel
비누		toothbrush
욕조		toothpaste
샤워		sink

p.151

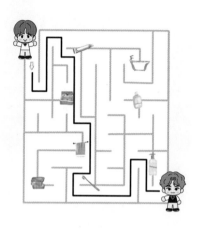

p.154

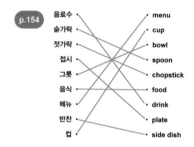

음료수		menu
숟가락		cup
젓가락		bowl
접시		spoon
그릇		chopstick
음식		food
메뉴		drink
반찬		plate
컵		side dish

p.158

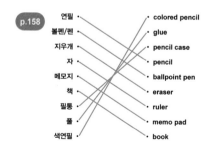

연필		colored pencil
볼펜/펜		glue
지우개		pencil case
자		pencil
메모지		ballpoint pen
책		eraser
필통		ruler
풀		memo pad
색연필		book

Answers 답안

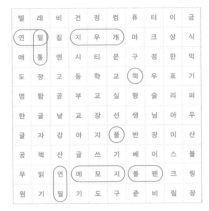

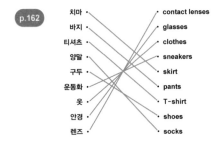

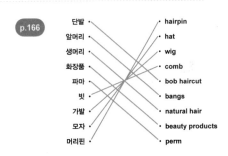

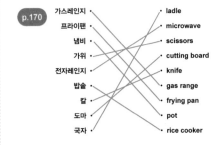

Answers 답안

p.171

프	스	팬	이	가	라

프	라	이	팬

전	국	솥	자	밥	칼

밥	솥

비	주	방	도	구	냄

냄	비

가	스	마	국	자	도

도	마

p.174

얼굴 •
눈 •
코 •
입 •
귀 •
손 •
발 •
팔 •
다리 •

• legs
• feet
• hands
• nose
• eyes
• arms
• mouth
• face
• ears

p.175

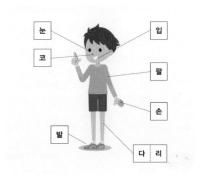

눈
코
입
팔
손
발
다 리

p.178

손바닥 •
손가락 •
발바닥 •
손톱 •
발가락 •
보조개 •
쌍꺼풀 •
눈썹 •
속눈썹 •

• eyelashes
• eyebrows
• double eyelids
• dimple
• palm
• fingers
• sole
• toes
• fingernails

p.179

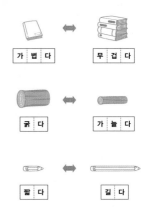

가	볍	다

무	겁	다

굵	다

가	늘	다

짧	다

길	다

p.184

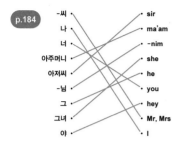

-씨	sir
나	ma'am
너	-nim
아주머니	she
아저씨	he
-님	you
그	hey
그녀	Mr, Mrs
야	I

p.188

엄마	younger sibling
아빠	older sister
할머니	older brother
할아버지	grandmother
누나	grandfather
형	mother
동생	father
언니	older brother (female)
오빠	older sister (female)

p.192

영화	musical
영화배우	ticket
입장권	movie
초대장	seat
좌석	book
연극	admission ticket
표	actor/actress
예매하다	invitation
뮤지컬	play

p.193

영화	를	좋아하다
표	를	준비하다
초대장	을	받다
좌석	에	앉다

p.196

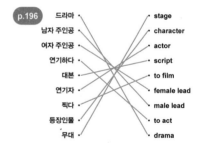

드라마	stage
남자 주인공	character
여자 주인공	actor
연기하다	script
대본	to film
연기자	female lead
찍다	male lead
등장인물	to act
무대	drama

p.197

〈주인공〉

주	공	인
인	주	공
공	인	주

〈연기자〉

자	연	기
기	자	연
연	기	자

〈초대장〉

장	대	초
초	장	대
대	초	장

〈입장권〉

권	장	입
장	입	권
입	권	장

p.205

상	상	하	다	연	습	생	시	절	쿤
굿	어	린	이	집	잘	생	기	다	대
모	가	죽	이	되	어	주	인	공	학
닝	초	등	학	교	마	크	유	치	원
도	서	실	장	문	무	대	오	르	다
서	울	초	대	학	교	의	댄	스	짱
관	우	등	생	은	연	습	스	스	로
텐	중	학	교	엔	고	등	학	교	실
도	서	관	에	가	는	날	원	장	님
시	티	하	이	스	쿨	일	이	칠	반

p.200

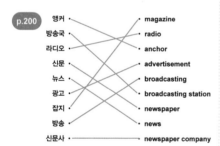

p.204

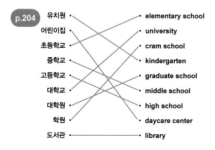

p.208

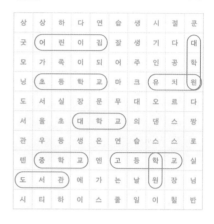

p.212

p.213

glass bottle	유 리 병
plastic bag	비 닐
paper	종 이
trash	쓰 레 기
recycling	재 활 용

p.216

한복 · · fan dance
한옥 · · palace
윷놀이 · · jegichagi
궁 · · hanbok
부채춤 · · hanok
제기차기 · · gat
떡국 · · Korean New Year
설날 · · rice cake soup
갓 · · yutnori

p.220

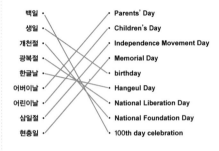

백일 · · Parents' Day
생일 · · Children's Day
개천절 · · Independence Movement Day
광복절 · · Memorial Day
한글날 · · birthday
어버이날 · · Hangeul Day
어린이날 · · National Liberation Day
삼일절 · · National Foundation Day
현충일 · · 100th day celebration

p.221

1. ❷   2. ❹   3. ❸   4. ❶